1. Ask God to bless and guide you as you consider what's most helpful to bring families in your community closer to him in the coming months.

2. Glance through the four sessions so that you have an overview of the months ahead, noting down resources that will take time to source.

3. Use the downloadable planning sheets to share this month's session with your core team in plenty of time to shape the ideas together to suit your own situation.

4. If you're meeting face to face with the team, talk about this month's theme, using the Messy team theme provided.

5. Tell God your worries.

6. Ensure that the whole extended team ha copies of your final version of activities, together with the Bible reflection provided to give them the background they need. You could give them the link to the passage on **biblegateway.com** if you're not certain they have their own Bibles.

7. Include take-home ideas on handouts, texts or a Facebook page.

CW01045503

…. ……. …… ….. you saw him at work.

Planning suggestions

Contents

Go to **messychurch.org.uk/ getmessymay19** to download all templates at A4 size, including a session planning sheet

In our next issue

September: God loves a cheerful giver

October: God's armour of light

November: Feast of faith

December: Small is mighty

Let's do this... together!

It's six years exactly since the first issue of *Get Messy!* appeared. And as this new year gets underway with the theme of *discipleship* running through every month, we're just about to go into our second International Conference, also on the theme of discipleship. When Messy Church began in 2004, 'discipleship' wasn't really something we had on our mind. (Pasta was.) It's a sign of the journey God's brought us on that the question of 'living as a Christian' has come so much to the fore since then, and has become one of the main concerns in our BRF team: how do we help people grow in Christ in and through Messy Church? How do people come closer to God and to each other? How does our Messy Church team grow? How do we discover 'life in all its fullness' unique to each person? Where does comfort stop and challenge start? How can we tell when someone starts walking the way of Christ? What can our church traditions teach us and what do we need to reimagine for today's society and for an all-age community?

It's a challenge that we've gladly taken up, knowing there's no way we can meet it solely in our limited resources at BRF, but delighting in the way we're discovering, as a global network, how we 'crack' this *together*. BRF acts as a catalyst, throws in resources, permissions, blessings, ideas, encouragement, opportunities to share and feed back, but the real pioneering and discovery happens in Messy Churches like yours: in Canada, South Africa or Germany, in the Methodist, Lutheran or URC church… (*Why not add your own country and denomination here?*) Jesus' invitation to join his rag-tag band of followers is one to grow closer to him in community, and you and I, my Messy friends, have the incredible gift of doing just that without any of the normal barriers of church tradition or national barriers: we're in this *together*.

Will we 'crack discipleship'? Is that even the right question? (Many of my church friends would wince at the idea of 'cracking discipleship' or even at calling the Christian life 'discipleship' in the first place.) Yes, we will. We can do this thing! I think we need to be robust and let the nuances look after themselves, afterwards. Once people in walking boots have trodden a path, those in flip-flops (or thongs, dear Aussie friends, but not UK ones for reasons of decency) can follow. We need to '*carpe* the *diem*', because we know exactly how short the '*diem*' can be for a child growing up, or a family moving on after a short sojourn in our area. So let's commit to working *together* to try out the ideas from the Discipleship Pilot and others of our own, and to sharing those results with the rest of the network through the BRF hub, so that everyone can benefit and together we can find a fruitful way forward. Let's communicate better what seems to work and what seems to be a failure or just a very slow boil. We can build up a body of wisdom that will be as robust as Messy Church itself, in order to bless those in all churches, not just in Messy Churches.

So how do the sessions in these 2019–20 magazines help? The session themes reflect the ten 'Holy Habits' Andrew Roberts explores in his book and resource materials of the same name: **prayer**, **making more disciples**, **worship**, **fellowship**, **gladness and generosity**, **biblical teaching**, **eating together**, **sharing resources**, **service** and **breaking bread**. The stories we explore are the usual range from the whole Bible, not just the 'easy' stories, as we try to be church for everyone. And the writers have given helpful inspiration, not just to wheel out a Messy machine, but to try out ways to enrich and deepen what we do and how we do it in the suggestions surrounding the actual activities: make the most of them!

To share your Messy Discipleship ideas and experiences, email **lucy.moore@brf.org.uk**

The impact of Messy Church

Jo Birkby, Children and Families Worker at Holy Trinity and St Saviour's Churches, Knaphill with Brookwood

Our Messy journey began over ten years ago, after a visit to St Wilfrid's in Cowplain, the founding place of Messy Church. Six months of prayer followed, our excitement mounting as we realised that this might be the breakthrough for which we'd been looking. Back then, our Sunday children's groups at St Saviour's were run by the parents of the children who came, and we were attracting no other families other than those who came to our once-a-month puppet service. Messy Church offered us another way of reaching out to local families who'd never thought of coming to church before.

Our 'launch' was at the local school fair. We gave them a taste of what Messy Church would look like on our stall, asked them if they'd come and on what day they'd prefer us to hold it. Saturdays were earmarked, and gallons of PVA and a tonne of glitter were purchased by amazing members of our church who 'got it' immediately and, what's more, wanted to join the team! And so began a journey that has been a rollercoaster ride, attracting a regular core of families whose children have grown with us and are now young leaders themselves.

Last year, we began a Messy mentoring scheme where these young leaders were invited to set up and test-run all of the activities before the 'big day' itself. It's been a great opportunity to share the Bible stories with them, help them grow in their relationship with Jesus and each other, and give them the skills and confidence they need not only to direct the activities but to engage in those all-important 'Messy' conversations. One of our young leaders, Chloe, who is just twelve years old, says, 'Becoming a young leader has really boosted my confidence and given me the skills to deal with challenging things now.' It's had an impact not just on her time at Messy Church but in so many other areas.

One of our Messy mums writes, 'Messy Church has been a part of our family life since we moved to Brookwood from Australia and first heard about it. Our children Rebecca, Amy and Zach have loved being involved each month with the creative activities (Zach particularly loves the edible ones!) and the Bible learning. For us, it's been a great way for them to experience truths about God, share prayers and learn with friends and the lovely Messy team. Rebecca and Amy have now both grown and moved on to being young leaders, which they love. They are so supported by a godly group of mentors and this is really special for me as well, knowing that they have these relationships.'

Regular contact with the children and families has been key. We meet at other times and places throughout the month in school lunch clubs, assemblies and cafes. Relationship is so vital to everything we do – and keeping Jesus at the centre so we can continually point to him, giving him the glory for all of our Messy endeavours!

As a leader, the impact Messy Church has had on my own life has also been immense. I began Messy Church as a church member and mum of two and, since then, I have been appointed as the Children and Families Worker for our parish. God has shown me what is possible when you're willing to take risks and are prepared to make changes to the way 'things have always been done'. It's been an incredible ten years and we look forward to the continuing adventure as we move into the next decade!

Discipling young people

Iain Nash, Children's Pastor, Southcourt Baptist Church, Aylesbury

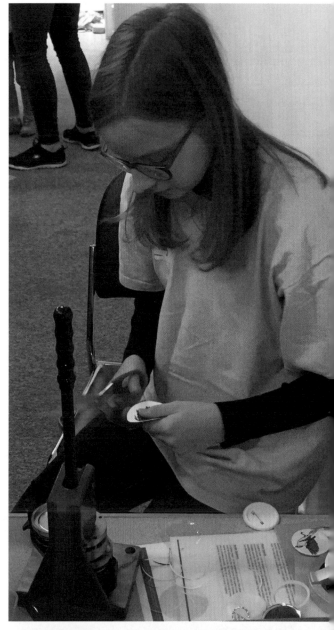

Messy Church Aylesbury has as many as 300 people who regularly attend from all over the local community. In order to be able to manage such numbers, we need a strong team in place that has plenty of energy and exuberance. What excites me the most is that the team is made up of a large contingent of young people from within our church family.

It is even more remarkable because, by rights, they should still be in bed when Messy Church Aylesbury happens, as we meet during the school holiday. However, we are always amazed at how willing they are to come along and serve so faithfully each time.

From helping on craft tables to manning bouncy castles and supervising computer consoles, the young people are given specific roles and responsibilities that match their skills and passions. We are blessed to have some wonderful artists among the young people who do face painting, as well as those who love drama, puppets and sound and visuals, all helping to bring the drama stories and songs that we do to life.

Where the young people really swing into action is the preparing and serving of our famous hot-dog lunch. As the families get into small groups to eat, the young people bring the food to the people and serve them. It can be really hard sometimes when you have nearly 300 hungry people desperately wanting their food, but the young people continue to serve with a smile and take joy and pride in providing for people in this way.

Once Messy Church has finished and those who came along have gone home, you will still find the young people clearing up and packing away. Mind you, there are hot dogs left to be eaten, always a good incentive to stay!

I really do believe that we must continue to give all young people opportunities like this. It excites me because this is exactly where I started my journey to becoming a Children's Pastor: as a fresh-faced young person who was asked if I would help at a church event like Messy Church. I grabbed the opportunity with both hands and never looked back. It excites me to see these young people responding in the same way that I did.

One of the many key characteristics of Jesus' training of the disciples was that he gave them tasks to do, commissioning them by giving them authority in the process and trusting them to do what he asked them to do. In the same way, I have done just that. I continue to model things to them, encourage them and point out improvements, but I never stop praying for them. Result? We see these young people become true disciples of Jesus Christ as they share him with people through their words and actions.

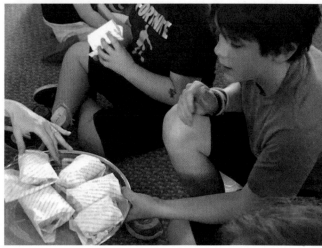

I pray this discipleship continues for years to come as they grow in their faith and as Messy Church Aylesbury sees Christ's kingdom grow on earth.

Seriously Messy

Making space for families to talk together about death and life

Victoria Slater, Project Researcher for Oxford Diocese

Seriously Messy (BRF, published June 2019) is designed to resource those who want to help families and people across all generations talk together about what our mortality and our encounters with death and dying might mean for how we choose to live out our lives and our faith.

It starts with the acknowledgement that, for all sorts of reasons, it's hard to talk about death and dying. However, this is part of life and the natural order, and we can't deal with it by avoiding it; we all know that we will have to face it for ourselves one day. It's good and healthy to be able to talk about it as a society and as individuals, and society is beginning to wake up to this fact.

For example, 'Death cafés', where people can come together to talk about death and dying over a coffee, are commonplace, and organisations such as the National Council for Palliative Care (**ncpc.org.uk**) and the Dying Matters Coalition (**dyingmatters.org**) have brought the topic of death and the process of dying back into the public arena. This is part of a wider recognition that we need to talk about death so that we can be practically prepared and better equipped to face up to it; familiarity reduces anxiety. Talking about death can also help make us more mature human beings who have a better chance of living life well, because we will have seen the bigger picture and gained a sense of perspective.

One of the important things about *Seriously Messy* is that it is for families. It recognises that we need to include children in our talk about death. This is for several reasons, including the basic fact that we can't prevent children from encountering death, for example, through the loss of a pet, grandparent, sibling, friend or parent. Although children are often exposed to death in unreal ways on TV, in video games or on social media, the physical reality of death can be totally unexpected and shocking. It's better to provide some wise resources than to leave children uninformed and without resources. People of any age experience death and loss, so it is important that we are able to talk about it together and, in so doing, support and equip people for whenever they encounter death in their life.

This book addresses the fact that, although the life, death and resurrection of Jesus Christ – the transformation of death to life – stands at the centre of the Christian faith, churches are not very good at making space for people to talk about what death and dying means to them. *Seriously Messy* puts talking about death in the context of the Christian faith by suggesting ways to make this space and offering relevant examples from the Bible. By engaging with death in this way, people can explore their questions and concerns, as well as being able to rediscover the hope of eternal life that is central to the Christian faith.

Seriously Messy helps people to explore fundamental issues such as: the messiness of life and death; the Christian message of life and hope in the midst of death and loss; and the need to include children and to take care about how we talk about death with them. It also looks at how leaders can take care of themselves when helping others to talk about this subject.

We have attempted a 'bottom-up' approach to the subject in the book. It accepts that everyone will come with different experiences, questions and understandings, both of death and dying and of the elements of the Christian faith. The approach that we advocate is to encourage honest conversations that involve wondering, reflecting, explaining, telling stories and, above all, listening. This way of approaching the subject can enable those involved to develop a deeper sense of the meaning of the hope of 'resurrection' and 'eternal life'. They will encounter different perspectives and understandings that may illuminate, enlarge or challenge their own. We also recognise that no one has all the answers. There is so much about death that is a mystery, that we will only understand when it comes to our own death. But we can live with the questions and explore them honestly together in the light of the gospel and, in so doing, enrich our lives and our faith. Perhaps we will even better prepare ourselves to meet the end of our own life, whenever and however it comes.

Seriously Messy is written by Joanna Collicutt, Lucy Moore, Martyn Payne and Victoria Slater, and is available from **brfonline.org.uk** from June 2019.

Messy Church (still) does science!

To find out more about Messy Church Does Science, visit **messychurch.org.uk/science**.

Is it really nearly two years since we first launched Messy Church Does Science? It must be time for a round-up of what people are saying… and if you haven't yet given it a go, grab a copy of the book and see where it takes you!

Our children love it. I borrow a child-size lab coat and goggles from the school, appoint our scientist of the month, who puts it on, and name him/her 'professor'. The professor then follows the instructions. It's great fun and the children are engaged in the Bible story.

Linda

It's always the 'best part' when we do a science activity, so now we try to fit one in every time. The older kids especially love it.

Bekki

I try to include some science every time. Boiled cabbage juice and 'acid' is popular, as well as growing beans, building balloon rockets, etc. In one of my churches, we are blessed to have our very own electrician, who built 'lemon batteries' with the kids (including using a very important-looking multimeter!). What especially pleases me is that it seems to appeal to girls and boys alike. I often use these activities to reflect on God's awesome creation and the importance of learning about and looking after it.

Melanie

We have done a number of scientific activities. Older boys and dads love them!

Alison

We do a science activity each time. It's amazing how you can link them to the themes. Lots of the children enjoy it. It's added another dimension and engaged those who don't particularly enjoy crafts.

Cath

When we do science, it's always popular!

Emma

We do it every time, now! We have a teenager scientist-in-residence. Not sure yet how much it is impacting for building faith, but the children love it! Makes for good variety.

Ann

We have tried to include a science activity in all our Messy Church events for a couple of years, now. We are in the excellent position of having a team member who is a retired Science Consultant for schools. She used to run numerous workshops and also trained teachers in delivering the science curriculum – so, as you can imagine, she has a great wealth of scientific knowledge linked with a wonderful faith. Her activities are always very enjoyable for the children and parents who attend Messy Church.

Sue

We are enjoying using Messy Science with our new Messy Young Leaders group.

Jane

Messy Café

Is there something missing from your Messy Church?

Dave Martin, Children, Youth & Families Coordinator Licensed Lay Minister, Christ Church & St John's, Radlett

I wonder if you can relate… You meet every month, with a beautifully committed team of individuals, armed with glue sticks, cake and an unwavering desire to reflect the love of Jesus to all around. However, each time you open your doors, you feel this urge to go deeper somehow. You want to go beyond crafts and truly cultivate an environment where intergenerational relationships enable both young and old to lead each other on in faith. If you're honest, you want so much more for your Messy Church, but getting there is hard.

Last year in Radlett, we challenged ourselves to look critically at what we were providing. After many prayer-fuelled team meetings and a lot of listening, we realised that, for us, the area for improvement was the base relationship between 'church' and 'wider community'. It's not fair to say that it wasn't there at all, but frankly we weren't as welcoming and relevant as we thought we were, and our Messy Church felt more like a children's club than an all-age congregation. Eek.

So, although we didn't know exactly what the future held, our amazing team said a big 'YES' in faith to our next challenge, and on 4 October 2017, we launched Messy Café! Since then, each week, we have transformed our church building into a community-focused café space where everybody is welcome, regardless of faith, background or circumstance.

For about a year and a half now, we have not only served hundreds of fairly traded lattes, over a thousand milkshakes and more slices of home-made cake than you could dream of, but we have also created a vibrant, life-giving space for the church and the wider community to grow in relationship together.

Although Messy Café is distinct from Messy Church, it is firmly connected to it and its vision. Messy Café is primarily about loving people like God loves us – through relationship – and Messy Church is more focused on who Jesus is, how our lives can be positively impacted by God, and how we can love him in return.

Each week, Messy Café meets at the same time and in the same place as Messy Church (except the fourth week, which is Messy Church) to ensure the two spaces are both familiar to and practical for most people. Inside, you'll find adults

[Messy Café is] a model based on relationships built through intentional conversations with key persons who are not only sociable, but also have a confident faith in Christ… Participation has been key and the intergenerational nature has been one that is encouraging… I love that it exemplifies mission – without having to be something stylised. A faith expression that is naturally inclusive.

Dean Pusey, Diocesan Youth Officer in St Alban's Diocese

connecting over a coffee, children doing activities and whole families spending quality time together. It's a drop-in space for all ages, and people can stay for the whole hour and a half, or just pop in for ten minutes.

For us in Radlett, Messy Café has provided a much-needed relational stepping stone for so many people on the discipleship journey through Messy Church, who now love being a part of the whole community. What was a gathering of 25 people once a month last year has turned into a vibrant community of (on average) 70 people each week. It's so wonderful to see what God has done and continues to do through it.

If you would like to explore the idea of running a Messy Café alongside your existing Messy Church, please feel free to contact Dave for more information, as he would love to explore with you how this could benefit your community: childrenandyouth@radlettchurches.org.uk; 01923 857998.

> Its drop-in ethos works really well for us.
>
> It has brought together the community.
>
> It has helped me to learn about Jesus.
>
> I want to tell more people about Messy Café and Messy Church.
>
> Children and adults at Messy Café

Four Messy Church values for Messy Café

As well being a Christ-centred environment, Messy Café is rooted in Messy Church's core values…

All-age: It should be a space where every age group WANTS to go, not where parents HAVE to go for the sake of their children.

Creativity: It should embrace the creative contributions of each individual. Like the body of Christ, every member should be encouraged to contribute their God-given gifts.

Hospitality: It should offer a high-quality service with a friendly, welcoming and relational environment. It's about reflecting Jesus' unconditional love and giving our absolute best, every time. So, bye-bye instant coffee, and hello filter!

Celebration: It should not only be a space where intergenerational relationships are celebrated, but where everyone feels able to share the messiness of life together; the joys, struggles, and questions of faith.

> Messy Café has opened our church doors to the community and provides a safe space where we are able to share God's goodness and love together. The welcoming and open atmosphere enables deep and meaningful conversations about the realities of life and how God might be part of it. We are so thankful to God.
>
> Revd Javaid Iqbal, Team Rector, Christ Church and St John's, Radlett

Companions for the journey: A Messy small-group experiment

Johanna Myers, Director of Christian Formation, Aldersgate UMC, South Carolina

Are we making disciples at Messy Church? Yes! Any time we invite people to join other disciples at work and play in God's kingdom, discipleship happens. After five years of doing Messy Church, though, I wondered, 'What would Messy Church look like as a small group?' In 2018, folks from Messy Church at Aldersgate United Methodist Church in Greenville, South Carolina took on this Messy experiment!

We formed small groups (six to ten people, or three to four families) that met monthly for a meal together, prayer and Bible study. The only catch? These groups would be intentionally multigenerational. No sending the kids off to play while the adults got down to the 'business' of Bible study. No lecturing adults telling kids what this Bible passage *has* to mean. These would be groups where all ages learn *together*. Group members would be companions for one another on their discipleship journey, so we called this experiment 'Companion groups'.

The five core values of Messy Church – hospitality, all-age, celebration, creativity, Christ-centred – form the Rule of Life for our Companion groups. A Rule is simply a guide that we've agreed on to help us navigate the messiness of life together. Companions promised to go beyond being a fellowship group to create space for encountering God in transforming ways. We promised to honour the gifts of everyone, from youngest to oldest, making room for everyone to lead and share. We promised to explore faith creatively and to be open to trying new things. We committed to meeting around a meal, extending hospitality to one another. All of this, we promised, was so that we might celebrate life together.

After a lively meal together – spent catching up with one another and sharing life – groups turn to study the month's Bible passage. Everyone, from youngest to oldest, is invited to ask questions and think creatively about the Bible. What do you notice about this story? What do you wonder about the people in the story? Where do you see yourself? After talking a bit about the story, groups get hands-on: playing a game, doing a craft or tackling a science experiment. Basically, groups do one activity that would be like an activity done at Messy Church. One month, a group built a labyrinth out of blocks as they talked about the walk to Emmaus. Another month, a group made bread and learned about Jesus feeding the 5,000. Groups planted seeds, painted and played together throughout the year. Each group chose their monthly activity, so it suited their own ages and strengths.

After a year of this Messy Discipleship experiment, what can we say about Messy Church and small groups? I am in awe of the depth of the relationships formed through Companion groups. It is a beautiful thing to see a four-year-old run up to her Companions because they have become like grandparents to her. It's rather amazing to see twelve-year-olds *EXCITED* about hanging out with a group of adults and looking forward every month to their Companion gathering. Relationships formed in Companion groups have been transformative.

On the other hand, I've also learned some hard truths about us adults! Many of our adults struggled a bit, especially early on, with the imaginative aspect of exploring

scripture together. They want answers, a lesson plan! Even after a year of following this same rhythm, I noticed that some adults still struggled with defaulting into 'lecture-mode'. When we do this, though, we miss out on what our kids have to share. And, trust me, our kids have so much insight and wisdom to offer!

Just as the activities help to ground a Messy Church, the hands-on activity grounded Companion groups. If we're going to have intergenerational groups where children feel included, the activity is *essential* – and interestingly, I learned through our experiment that groups which spent too much time *talking* about the story lost the kids' attention quickly.

This Messy Discipleship project is still a work in progress for us. What I can say is that the core values and model of Messy Church do work well together as the basis for small groups, for Messy Churches wanting to dive deeper into new ways of growing as disciples.

For more information about Companion groups and our discipleship experiment, feel free to contact me at: **jmyers@aumcsc.org**.

Youth column

Eleanor Bloxham

I am a creative person. I love making things: painting, crochet, clay-modelling, bottle rockets powered by methylated spirits – it's all so much fun! Creativity is an important part of Messy Church as one aspect of the activities, but it's also there in the celebration, in how you express hospitality and in making it accessible to a whole range of ages. Creativity can also be an expression of worship and a great reminder that we are made in the image of our creator God.

Messy Church has a fantastic ability to say that you are welcome and you are loved, even if other church services don't suit you or you want something that your family can do together. It is such a joy to be able to learn about God with all ages through creative activities – and that you can engage with and explore the stories with the people you have come with, people you have just met or people that you have only got to know through Messy Church. The relationships that are developed here and while sharing food are key to building the sense of community that many in Messy Church feel. When I found that Messy Church BRF were looking for another intern, that is why I wanted the job.

I spent the last few years studying Chemistry and so am thrilled to be part of the Messy Church Does Science project, joining in with the roadshows and science training events. Science is great fun at any age – especially when you don't have to do any homework! You may go away from our science activities slightly damp or smelling of vinegar, but I guarantee you will have had the chance to enjoy experimenting and probably learned a bit about how the world works, too. I think science in Messy Church is a significant asset as it provides great scope for creativity and allows us to get to know the world we live in and the God that created it.

I have been a part of Messy Church in Christ Church with All Saints Blackpool since 2014, along with my mum (who does a lot of the planning), my dad (who comes up with science-based activities like volcanoes or magnetic fishing) and my grandma (who helps in the kitchen). I have really enjoyed my involvement in all aspects of helping Messy Church sessions happen. It has been encouraging to see the growth of our Messy Church and the responses of the families that attend regularly.

This year, I moved to Nottingham and have been working with three Messy Churches at St Wilfrid's Calverton, St Andrews Skegby and All Saints Stanton Hill. Working with these churches, which all operate in different situations, and visiting other Messy Churches, has been really interesting as it has helped me to see how different Messy Churches are adapted to fit the needs of the people who attend. I have also had the chance to speak to many people about their own experience of Messy Church and, from this, have found out favourite songs, favourite foods and how to set up Messy Church in all sorts of different spaces!

Over my year with Messy Church, I have been researching Messy Churches on urban estates to find out more about the joys and challenges of working in this context, with an aim to discover if there is more we could do to better support these Messy Churches. We also hope that this research will be useful to anyone who is thinking about starting or is already running a Messy Church in this setting and to the people who support them.

The lowdown on Messy Vintage

Debbie Thrower, team leader of The Gift of Years

'It's too much fun to be kept for the young, isn't it?' enthused a curate, chatting to me about Messy Vintage. This latest form of Messy Church, specifically for people in the second half of life, is taking off... fast!

Messy Vintage services are happening on the south coast in Dorset, parts of Hampshire and Sussex, as well as in Surrey, Kent and Essex – and these are just the ones we know about. We're finding new churches every week who tell us they're giving it a go. A man piped up at a meeting in Crickhowell, in the Brecon Beacons, to add, 'We're doing Messy Vintage in the care homes around Abergavenny.'

Just as Messy Church is 'all age', its missional offshoot Messy Vintage, supported by BRF programme The Gift of Years, attracts volunteers in their 50s and 60s-plus, while those attending are typically in their 80s, 90s and even 100s. That represents five- or six-decades' worth of all-age worship!

The trend has even reached New Zealand. The Revd Ruth Dewdney explains how her Anglican church, in the Bay of Plenty, Te Puke, has just held its first Messy Vintage in the dementia unit of a facility for the care of older people, called Carter House.

'We had twelve of the fifteen residents involved, plus helpers from the parish, plus staff. We are planning on holding a Messy Vintage each month, then afternoon tea with the residents.'

Whether at home in the UK or abroad, Messy Vintage always ends with food – usually tea and cakes – or, if taking place in a care home, some services end with grace before residents depart for lunch or high tea in their own dining room.

Above all, it is fun and creative. It brings older people together for worship, craft and discussions around our messy, but special, lives. Even when later life brings challenges, joining together for fellowship in this way helps everyone glimpse the ways God is alongside us at every age and stage, even in the sometimes chaotic times in our old age.

BRF offers twelve free session plans for anyone wanting to know how to get started. There are scarecrows to be made at Harvest time, mini maps of the world to fashion with an environmental theme and mosaic tiles to be created, which remind us how we can meet Jesus in unexpected places. These can be downloaded online at **thegiftofyears.org.uk/ messy-vintage-sessions**.

Key to Messy Vintage is that:

- It helps older people know they are part of something bigger
- It's about being 'a blessing' and being 'blessed' by others
- Worship often releases the voice of older people; this is church for the voiceless
- It's about a church creating sacred space where people are
- The food should be as beautiful as the people involved.

What began in Jersey has – thanks to pioneer Katie Norman, the National Coordinator, and a little help from The Gift of Years team – started catching on as word spreads from place to place. Salvation Army Major Sharon King wrote to tell us how she got involved:

'As I was leading worship one Sunday, I suddenly came to the realisation that a lot of my congregation did not know the basic Bible stories and so I began a monthly Messy Vintage for adults. A time of devotion would commence; I used stories from Godly Play, which were well-received, and quite a few of the ten folk who attended commented over time that seeing the Bible come alive in this way helped them to understand more about the scriptures. I shall never forget one Friday afternoon when I made an altar call and four people made a commitment to Christ.'

In conjunction with other Christian charities, BRF's Messy Vintage is also encouraging churches to 'Make a meal of it'. This is an initiative of Christians Together Against Loneliness (of which The Gift of Years is a member). The idea is simple: use a meal event to reach out to the older people in your community.

What better way to 'Make a meal of it' than to put on a Messy Vintage session, which then moves seamlessly into a hearty meal for those who'd welcome a little bit of TLC, some warm company and quality hospitality?

The details of how to plan such an event, a leaflet explaining what's what and our helpful top-tips factsheet can all be downloaded at **thegiftofyears.org.uk/messy-vintage**.

Don't forget our Pinterest page, either, with its growing 'virtual noticeboard' of tried-and-tested ideas to suit all abilities right across the ageing spectrum: **pinterest.co.uk/ MessyChurchBRF/messy-vintage**.

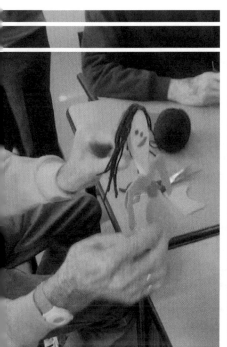

#discipleship: team

We're bringing out a new discipleship resource specially for Messy Church teams and other lay leaders, providing a month's worth of daily reading notes focused around the Messy Church values. Publishing in June, *God's Word for Messy People* contains 31 short Bible passages, with a reflection on each passage by Lucy Moore, reinforcing the creativity, hospitality, joy, inclusivity and character of Jesus.

And for wider thinking around discipleship and how it plays out in Messy Church, Paul Moore's classic *Making Disciples in Messy Church*, reprinted with a refreshed cover, is a must-read for your team.

Visit **brfonline.org.uk** to get your copy!

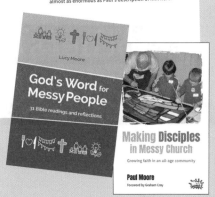

Mothers' Union gets messy!

Catherine Kyte, Faith Officer at Mothers' Union

Back in 2009, Lucy Moore spoke at a Mothers' Union (MU) Conference about Messy Church, at that time in its infancy, and we were blown away by what she shared! Since then, many of our members have plunged into Messiness in their local areas, embracing the concept with gusto!

Of course they have – the values behind Messy Church totally line up with the vision and mission of MU. We are proudly known for our hospitality as we wield the tea urn with purpose, providing welcome, a listening ear and a safe space alongside physical sustenance. As for craft – MU sees this this as a ministry, rather than just an activity!

And encouraging faith in the family has always been a key part of our aims and objectives, ever since our founder, Mary Sumner, made the first hesitant step in 1876 to gather mothers of all classes in her parish to help the women support one another in raising their children. A vital part of this was the encouragement to nurture their families in the love of God.

So fast-forward to today, and we see our members getting involved with Messy Church in a variety of ways as our shared aims weave themselves together. Penny Northall, from Derby Diocese, gives a great illustration of this:

> **Mothers' Union members of Hognaston and Hulland branch have skills and gifts that they bring to Hulland's Messy Church. These might be in creativity, cooking, listening, welcoming, leading or planning. The aims are the same for MU and Messy Church – 'sharing God's love with families'.**

Then, on a larger scale, MU and Messy Church have joined together at Liverpool Cathedral for Messy Palms on Palm Sunday, where children and adults enjoyed crafts, activities, worship and a picnic; and for the Mothering Sunday service 'Mother Love', where Messiness was the order of the day. The seasonal theme has continued, with MU taking part in the Messy Nativity Advent project; while Southwell and Nottingham members celebrated Lady Day in 2018 along very Messy principles, with all ages enjoying creative activities and prayer ideas together (some of which used chocolate – a winner!).

And the connections between us grow even stronger as we see the similarities we share on a global level. Since 1876, MU has grown to four million members in 84 countries – all of which are caring for families and nurturing faith in their own cultural context. As Messy Church has already started to expand into other countries, the potential for global partnership is beginning to take shape. Now that's an exciting thought!

Bev Jullien, the CEO of Mothers' Union, sums up the joy of the links we share:

> **The aims and values of MU and Messy Church align very well, so it's wonderful to work together for the good of families and the growth of God's kingdom.**

May our partnership together become increasingly Messy as we live out our shared vision to nurture faith in the family in ever more creative ways!

£100 Appeal

Messy Church helps people follow Jesus

Mona's story

Faith and community for all ages

Last year, we received a lovely photo from a Messy Church leader in a small village in Scotland. It showed Mona, a centenarian, cradling eight-month-old Alister in her arms. Mona is a regular at Messy Church and loves being part of the family. Every month, she goes along to have a chat, join in the activities and, of course, see her buddy, Alister!

The leader of Mona's Messy Church recalled how one afternoon they were exploring the story of Moses and the burning bush. The noisiest table was not one with children, but a group of adults colouring in a burning bush and all talking at once. At the centre of that group was Mona, chatting and smiling away and giving it her all because faith and community are important at all stages of life.

The Bible Reading Fellowship (BRF) is the home of Messy Church and we're a little younger than Mona, but not by much. Since 1922, we've been helping children and adults of all ages explore Christianity and grow in faith. We believe we have something to offer to everyone, whether you're a centenarian like Mona or a babe in arms like Alister.

Today, our creative programmes and resources impact thousands of lives across the UK and overseas, and Messy Church is one area where we've seen astounding growth and development. Every month, a staggering 500,000 are estimated to attend Messy Church. Some go to a Messy Church in a village, like Mona. Others meet in big cities and their suburbs or schools, care homes and even prisons.

Wherever it's found, the aim of Messy Church is the same: to help people become followers of Jesus. We regularly hear that children and adults of all ages are taking this important step because of what they've seen and experienced at Messy Church. It's fantastic news and something of which we are justly proud.

If you want to see more people coming to faith because of Messy Church, would you consider leaving a gift in your will to BRF? Legacies are an important source of income for us and we value every gift, small or large.

For more information about making a lasting difference through a gift in your will to BRF, please visit **brf.org.uk/ lastingdifference**, email **enquiries@brf.org.uk** or call us on **01865 319700**.

Session material: May

Holy Habit: Prayer

 Go to messychurch.org.uk/getmessymay19 to download all templates at A4 size, including a session planning sheet

#discipleship: individual

Messy reflection by Lindsey Goodyear

Jesus told his disciples a story. He wanted to show them that they should always pray and not give up. He said, 'In a certain town there was a judge. He didn't have any respect for God or care about what people thought. A widow lived in that town. She came to the judge again and again. She kept begging him, "Make things right for me. Someone is treating me badly."

'For some time the judge refused. But finally he said to himself, "I don't have any respect for God. I don't care about what people think. But this widow keeps bothering me. So I will see that things are made right for her. If I don't, she will someday come and attack me!"'

The Lord said, 'Listen to what the unfair judge says. God's chosen people cry out to him day and night. Won't he make things right for them? Will he keep putting them off? I tell you, God will see that things are made right for them. He will make sure it happens quickly. But when the Son of Man comes, will he find people on earth who have faith?'

Luke 18:1–8 (NIRV)

When I was a child, I used to write letters to my great-grandmother. Although it took some time for each letter to make its way to her, and then for her response to make its way back, it was worth the eager anticipation when I'd check the mail and see her letter. I'd swiftly read it, tuck it away with the others and get busy writing another. I was disciplined in my determination to stay in close contact with her despite the distance between us.

We live in different times, now. Gone are the days of handwritten letters that outline the details of our daily lives and events. Instead, we can pass along a short, impersonal email to anyone, anywhere around the world, and, once they've written their own quick response, mentally check a box as though we've held a great conversation.

The widow was diligent in her quest for justice. She never wavered despite the fact that the judge was unjust and unwilling to meet her requests. The judge openly says he doesn't fear God, nor does he respect anyone. He has no patience for the nagging widow until she finally wears him down and, out of annoyance, he gives up and gives her what she wants. She is exactly what God wants us to be.

The widow is the antithesis of what communication is today. There is no instant gratification for her. Instead, like the way God calls us to pray to him, she is persistent, knowing what she wants and waiting patiently for her request to be answered. These are the two words we should be focusing on: persistence and patience. We aim to be persistent in our prayer and communication with him, and patient for how and when he answers these prayers.

For a world now used to instant gratification, this is a seemingly impossible task. We want things done now. So praying persistently and waiting for our own 'justice' is going to take practice. Although it's hard to admit, in many cases we can relate better to the unjust judge. It's easier to think only of ourselves and forget about prayer at a time when we feel on top of the world or untouched by burden. However, we need to remember that praying consistently does not mean prayer only in a time of crisis. We cannot send an email to God and expect a response within the hour. So, instead, we have to practise the same amount of determined prayer as the widow in order to find satisfaction with our own life cases, no matter what the status of our life at the moment.

Like the determination and diligence I had for staying in communication with my great-grandmother, I will endeavour, like the widow, to stay unwavering in prayer and keep striving for the same communication with God. Will you join me?

#discipleship: team

Messy health check

How important is prayer to my life?

Messy team theme

- How can we make sure that prayer still stays top of our agenda when it comes to all the preparations for and busyness of running a Messy Church?
- What sorts of unfairness might drive us to pray for the people of our community?
- How can we remember to keep on praying for each other and for those who come to our Messy Church once the session is over?
- Encourage each other with stories of how God has answered prayer because God is a faithful judge.

Pray, pray, pray! by Martyn Payne

How does this session help people grow in Christ?

This parable shows us what God is not like – the unfair judge – but also what we are not like – the persistent widow. God is passionately concerned about unfairness in this world and longs for us to talk to him about it so that justice is done. Giving up on prayer is so easy and being unmoved by injustice around us is widespread; and being faithless about God's power to change things is a temptation for us all. God is just, and he calls us to be prayerful. This session is an opportunity to think about how important prayer is for us and for our families, and to recommit to praying about injustice.

#discipleship: families

Mealtime card

- When was the last time you said, 'It's not fair'?
- What's been the best way of sorting out unfairness in your family?
- What makes it hard for you to remember to pray?
- When is your best time to pray?

Take-home idea

Challenge yourselves to add a routine to your day, namely the habit of prayer. Talk together as a family about when the best time would be to do this together or on your own. Turn a paper plate into a clock face and decide on your special prayer moment in the day, filling in the hands of the clock to say when that will be. Make one clock face for yourself to keep in your room and one for the family which you stick up prominently somewhere.

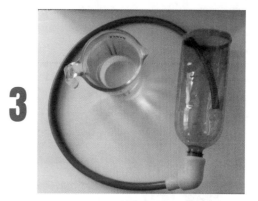

Question to start and end the session

So… if I dared to pray more, what difference would it make?

#discipleship: extra

Decide on a particular justice issue that affects your community or a part of the world with which you have links. Make this a prayer focus for all at Messy Church over the coming months, by setting up an information board with ideas for writing letters, campaigning, raising money and of course prayer.

Social action

Have a selection of local, national and international social projects' leaflets and invite families to take one away to pray for at home.

Session material: May

6

7

8

9

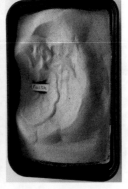

10

Activities

1. Widows' weeds

You will need: scissors; A3 black or dark-coloured paper; black plastic bin bags cut up into squares

Widows used to wear special clothes to show they were in mourning. Fold the paper into a party hat (find instructions online). Fold the plastic bag over and over lengthways concertina-style and then cut out holes at regular intervals so that, unfolded, it becomes a veil with lots of holes in it. Trap the veil under the cap to become your widows' weeds.

Talk about whether you know anyone in your community who has recently been bereaved. How can you show you care?

2. Headgear for the judge

You will need: a variety of cheap striped cloths; broad Kylie-band elastic sweatbands or white strips of cloth; felt-tip pens

Use felt-tip pens to decorate the bands and cloths. Attach the 'judge's headgear' with the bands. You could use this headgear when retelling the story in the celebration.

Talk about what guidelines you would use to try and work out what is fair and just.

3. Perpetual prayer

You will need: strong scissors; sticky tape; water; a large two-litre water bottle; one-metre length of tubing; stopper

Cut off the bottom of the emptied bottle. Make good any sharp edges with tape. Turn the bottle upside down and attach the tubing to the stopper. Arrange for the tube to go below the bottle and then up one side, before finally being directed back towards the newly cut-open end of the bottle.

Pour water from a jug into the opened bottle. Gravity and water pressure should push the water through the tubing and back up the tube and out to keep refilling the bottle! You will need to experiment with this, making sure there are no leaks and finding the right volume of water to make it work. How long can you keep the water going in a cycle?

Talk about how we can keep on praying and not give up, as Jesus asks of us.

f p t @MessyChurchBRF **Photocopying not permitted except under the CLA Church Licence.**

Pray, pray, pray! by Martyn Payne

4. Not giving up

You will need: needles and thread; balloons; ribbon, scissors; empty boxes

Try the following challenges: threading a needle; blowing up a balloon and then tying a knot in the end (or tie a knot in a string if you want to avoid using plastics); creating a perfect bow around a box (add more ideas if you like). Will people persist or feel like giving up?

Talk about what it feels like to have to keep on trying. Why do we find it so difficult to keep praying to God?

5. Justice for the widow!

You will need: pieces of card; bamboo sticks; sticky tape; paints; paint brushes; water bowls

Create your own campaign placard on behalf of the widow, painting and illustrating slogans such as: 'Justice now'; 'Just be fair, hear her prayer'; 'What do we want? Widows' rights.' Attach the placards to the sticks.

Talk about how far you would be prepared to go to campaign for justice for someone else.

6. Hanging in the balance

You will need: two 2-litre water bottles; a coat-hanger (preferably with hooks at the end of its arms); scissors; hole punch; pieces of string

Cut off the top part of your bottles neatly, taking care to leave no sharp edges. Using five long pieces of string for each bottle, tie them so that the knot sits beneath the base of the bottle and the ends of the string come up the side, through five holes that you make with a hole punch beneath the upper rim of each bottle. Tie the loose ends of the string together so the bottle hangs evenly. Hook the strings over the end of the coat hanger, one bottle on each side.

You now have home-made scales and can experiment putting things into the bottles so that each side balances the other.

Talk about how God can help us to make good judgements about things that happen to us in our everyday lives.

7. Prayer snacks

You will need: Hula Hoops; cream cheese; crackers; paper plates; plastic knives

Spread the cream cheese on three crackers and then use the hula hoops to create the letters A, S, K, placing one letter on each cracker. Just as the occasional snack during the day can give us energy to keep going, prayer is a vital ingredient to our lives that we need to exercise anywhere, any time.

Talk about what you are praying about at the moment.

8. Just keep praying!

You will need: cardboard tubes; sticky tape; small marbles/dried chickpeas; large board; plastic container

Create a marble run by cutting the tubes in half, making a hole at the end (to enable the marble to drop through) and attaching the tubes into each other in a downhill zigzag pattern supported by a backboard. Place a container at the bottom of the run and then set the marbles rolling down. As soon as one arrives at the bottom, pick it up and re-feed it into the system. How long can you keep the supply of marbles running down? You will certainly need help from others.

Talk about the sort of things that help us keep praying.

9. Prayers for justice

You will need: lots of mission and aid magazines; a tabletop map of the world; scissors; glue sticks

Find headlines and/or photos of situations of injustice in our world from the magazines. Cut out and glue them to map of the world, pausing to say a simple prayer asking God to help.

Talk about what God might be asking us to do about some of these situations.

10. Finding faith

You will need: shallow trays; labels; coloured marker pens; sand

Write the word 'Faith' on labels and attach them in several places on the base of the trays, sometimes at an angle and sometimes upside down but with plenty of space in between the words. Cover the words with the sand to a depth of 3 or 4 cm. Invite those who come to the table to hunt around in the sand in the trays for the word 'faith' without any of the sand spilling out of the tray.

Talk about what keeps you trusting in God. What encourages you to pray?

Session material: May
Pray, pray, pray! by Martyn Payne

Celebration

The two big things in today's Messy Church have been prayer and justice. Hands up if you've ever said, 'It's not fair!' Hands up if you've ever been angry that someone else has been cheated or badly treated.

God has given us a strong sense of right and wrong because that's what God is like. God is always completely fair. This world badly needs justice. Hands up if you've ever tried praying. Hands up if you've found it hard.

God has put into all of us an instinct to pray but so much seems to get in the way and we easily give up. Jesus once told a story about prayer and justice.

Invite adults and children who made widows' weeds, judges' headgear or placards to go and collect them to help you tell the parable.

In the story there was a bad judge *(gather some of those dressed in judges' headgear and ask them to stand on one side of you)*, a judge who didn't care about being fair. He couldn't care less! *(The judges should all turn their backs on everyone, with arms folded and look grumpy.)*

And in the story there was a widow *(gather some of those dressed in widows' weeds and ask them to stand on the other side of you)*, a widow who had been treated very badly. For her, life was just not fair. She wanted justice. Day after day she brought her case to the judge. *(Gather some of those with placards on behalf of the widow and ask him to stand in front of you.)* She never stopped asking the judge to hear her case. *(Ask the 'campaigners' to chant the words on their placards and to get louder and louder.)*

But the judge kept on ignoring the widow. The shouts from the widow got louder and louder. It went on for weeks! *(Encourage the 'campaigners' and the widow to up their cry for justice.)*

Finally the judge grew so angry *(invite the judges to act in response to your words)* that he turned towards the widow... stamped his feet angrily... sighed very loudly... shook his fist fiercely... and cried out, 'STOP,' at the top of his voice. 'I give up', he said, 'you can have justice. Now please go away!'

(Everyone should return to their places.)

The bad judge listened to the widow in the end because she never gave up. I want you to be like the widow and not give up with prayer. But it's much better news for you because God is a good judge and will always listen and answer your prayers. So pray, pray, pray... God wants there to be fair play in the world, between all peoples, in every family and in each one of our lives.

We take it for granted that we look after our bodies. We make sure our eyes, ears, noses, tongues and hands are all working properly! We want all our senses in tip-top condition. God has given us our bodies and we need to look after them. But God has also given us prayer muscles – to talk with and listen to God... and these need exercising too. This story is saying that we need to make sure we pray regularly because that's the way God made us. And, more importantly, God has loads of answers to give us that are just waiting for our prayers. So pray, pray, pray!

(There is another celebration idea for this parable in *Messy Parables*, BRF, 2017.)

Prayer

Jesus promises that when we ask, seek and knock in prayer, God will answer us. Invite people to work in twos or threes to create, one at a time, human sculptures of the following capital letters: A, S and K. When each letter is formed, ask everyone to freeze and be still for each of the following prayers in turn.

Help us, Father God, to **ask** for your help every single day.

Help us Lord Jesus, to **seek** justice for those who are caught up in the unfairness of life.

Help us, Holy Spirit, to **knock** on heaven's door and welcome you into our lives every day. And all the people said AMEN

Song suggestions

'Ask, ask, ask' – Junior Praise
'Prayer is like a telephone' – Kidsource
'Lord, we cry' – Kidsource

Meal suggestion

Eating with hands, which can also of course be used to pray, would make a connection to the theme, so why not serve up tacos with a variety of fillings which individuals can fold in for themselves? You might also like to introduce pretzels as a snack dessert on the tables, with their prayer shape (hands crossed over the heart), familiar to the baker monks who invented them.

Session material: June
Dazzling disciples by Jocelyn Czerwonka

Holy Habit: Making Disciples

Go to messychurch.org.uk/getmessymay19 to download all templates at A4 size, including a session planning sheet

#discipleship: individual

Messy reflection by Anne Offler and Sharon Pritchard

After this, the word of the Lord came to Abram in a vision: 'Do not be afraid, Abram. I am your shield, your very great reward.'

But Abram said, 'Sovereign Lord, what can you give me since I remain childless and the one who will inherit my estate is Eliezer of Damascus?' And Abram said, 'You have given me no children; so a servant in my household will be my heir.'

Then the word of the Lord came to him: 'This man will not be your heir, but a son who is your own flesh and blood will be your heir.' He took him outside and said, 'Look up at the sky and count the stars – if indeed you can count them.' Then he said to him, 'So shall your offspring be.'

Abram believed the Lord, and he credited it to him as righteousness.

Genesis 15:1–6 (NIV)

Abram seems to be in an impossible situation. He and his wife, Sarai, are old and they have no children. Abram is sad, as he spends time talking to God, he hears something amazing. God promises that the impossible will happen, that he and his wife will have a son. God uses the wonderful example of the stars in the sky to reassure Abram that his descendants will be as numerous as the stars. Even though this sounds impossible, Abram trusts God. He believes what God says and, as the following chapters in the Bible tell us, God's word came true.

Part of being a disciple today, as it has always been, is to trust God, to listen to him and believe in the things he says and the guidance he gives. This is sometimes a challenge as, like Abram, God seems to ask, suggest or promise the impossible. We are still called to trust him. Sometimes things around us look impossible to change, have no obvious solution or seem very unlikely. As the stars twinkle and shine in this Bible reading, we too are asked to shine in the world, especially in impossible situations and with difficult people. We are asked to trust God and to share his love with others so they can be encouraged to trust him too and become one of his disciples. Abram's descendants were many like the stars in the sky, and we, along with other Christian disciples, are some of their number. I wonder if, when we encounter the seemingly impossible, we can shine even brighter.

#discipleship: team

Messy health check

Take a moment to name the people in whose lives you've seen God at work through your Messy ministry over the last few months.

Messy team theme

- Are we dazzling disciples, showing and sharing God's love with the people we meet?
- As a team exercise and preparation, do the Acrostic Disciple Challenge (activity 1). Brainstorm what it means to be a disciple of Christ.

How does this session help people grow in Christ?

This session helps people understand what a disciple is and to realise that we are all called to be disciples of Christ. Just like the stars shine to brighten up the dark sky, so too can we as disciples bring God's light to the world and the people we encounter. We can dazzle like a star if we are filled with God's love and share that love with those around us.

#discipleship: families

Mealtime card

- Could you be a dazzling disciple?
- What do you think a dazzling disciple looks like?
- Who do you know who would really like to be dazzled by the good news of Jesus?

Take-home idea

Let the stars remind you about being a dazzling disciple. At home, make stars to attach to your bedroom ceiling or make a star mobile. Write messages on them to remind you of what a dazzling disciple might do and look like. How can you be a

Session material: June

dazzling disciple for God? Think about others who would like to be dazzled by God's love. Maybe add their names to your stars and pray for them at night. Perhaps you could think about inviting them to the next Messy Church.

Question to start and end the session

So… can I be a dazzling disciple for Christ?

#discipleship: extra

Plan a Messy Outdoors event to reach people even Messy Church doesn't reach.

Social action

Tell the story of someone in your church who is a 'star' in all they do for social action.

1

3

4

5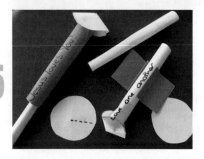

Activities

1. Acrostic disciple challenge

You will need: notice board; pins; nine pages of A4 paper; smaller pieces of coloured paper; pens

Using A4 paper, write each letter of the word 'DISCIPLES' on a separate piece of paper. Pin these at the top of a large notice board. On the strips of coloured paper, ask people to write under each letter words (beginning with that letter) relating to being a disciple e.g. D – Devoted. Pin them in columns to the board. See how many words people can come up with. See how long the list gets! Or take it further:

1. Choosing one word from anywhere in each column, see if you can make an interesting sentence working across from left to right e.g. Devoted – Inspirational – Servants – Committed – In – Prayer – Lovingly – Engaging – Spontaneously.

2. You can also work down a column and see if you can come up with alliteration – using at least four words starting with the same letter e.g. Daring disciples dutifully dedicated to God, or People pondering prayerful promises proclaiming peace poetically.

Talk about how Jesus calls us all to be his disciples. A disciple is a dedicated follower of Jesus. We can do this in our everyday lives sharing God's love with the people we meet, praying, being in fellowship with other Christians, breaking bread together and learning from the scriptures.

2. Bread making

You will need: pre-prepared bread dough; paper plates; baking trays; oven facilities

Have some pre-prepared bread dough ready to work and divide into small ball shapes. Shape dough as you like, maybe into people or the first letter of your name. Place on baking tray for baking and sharing together at meal or celebration time.

As Christians, we need to develop these Holy Habits such as breaking bread together. At the last supper, Jesus broke bread with his disciples and told them to 'do this in memory of me' (Luke 22:19, GNT).

Talk about how we can remember Jesus every time we eat or break bread.

Additional copies can be purchased at **brfonline.org.uk/9780857467751** or using the order form on page 39.

Dazzling disciples by Jocelyn Czerwonka

3. Woven stars

You will need: a selection of coloured A4 paper cut into strips; scissors

New Zealand is in the Southern Hemisphere, where some Messy Churches will be acknowledging Matariki (Maori New Year) with the rising of the constellation of stars called Pleiades. It is traditional to weave 'Harakeke whetu' (a flax star) as part of this celebration. Let's just start with paper stars. Choose four different colours, one of which you want to represent how God your creator is woven into your life.

Follow this link for instructions to make an eight-point Matariki Star: **youtube.com/watch?v=kZf5ewNd-q4**.

Talk about how we can never count the number of stars, as much as we may try. But stars are a reminder that our work as disciples is never finished; there are always more disciples to be made. As we weave the stars today, reflect on how much you allow God to be woven into your life in order for you to be a shining disciple of Jesus. How might you shine like a star to be a disciple of God?

4. Stargazing with Abram/Abraham

You will need: a darkened room or gazebo; cushions; cardboard stars; scripture verses printed out on paper (download online); string; safety pins; torches; clipboards; quiz sheets (download online); pens; dark cloth or black polythene for canopy

'The Lord took him outside and said, "Look at the sky and try to count the stars; you will have as many descendants as that"' (Genesis 15:5, GNT). If it's a fine night and dark where you are, go outside and see how many stars you can count. Alternatively, make your own stargazing room and use this quiz.

Before the session, paste printed scriptures (enlarged font) on to the cardboard stars. Use string and safety pins to hang stars from the canopy.

As people arrive, hand out torches and clip boards with quiz sheet and pens. Encourage them to take their time answering the questions and reflecting on what God might be saying to them.

Talk about whether or not you were surprised to learn that God had decided the number of stars and knows them all by name. Just as God knows the stars by name, so he knows us each by name.

5. Rocket disciples

You will need: pencils; felt-tip pens; paper straws or paper strips, thick pencils and sticky tape; paper; scissors; coloured Post-it notes

As Jesus' disciples, what messages would you like to send around the world on your rocket?

Use paper straws or make your own by rolling 6 cm x 20 cm paper strips lengthwise around a thick pencil. Tape edges and remove the pencil. Wrap a bit of tape around the bottom edge so it doesn't get soggy when blowing through it.

Make your rockets using 12 cm x 6 cm paper strips. Write lengthwise the message you would like to send, e.g. 'You are loved by God'. Decorate the rocket, and then wrap it around your straw and tape in place. Add wings using small Post-it notes; fold along the sticky edge and stick to the rocket.

Tape a 'cap' to the rocket. Using a lid about 5.5cm in diameter, draw a circle on paper and cut out. Mark a dot in the centre, rule a line from centre to edge and cut. Slide the edges to form a cone shape, tape edges and tape it to your rocket.

Now fly your rocket by inserting your straw and blowing through it. See how high it will go! Be careful not to aim at people.

Talk about what special messages you think Jesus would want us to send to people today.

6. Praying for Messy Churches all over the world

You will need: large map of the world; print-out or poster of countries and their flags; flags on toothpicks; Blu Tack. For a list of countries where Messy Churches can be found around the world, see messychurch.org.uk/international#countries.

Find the flags belonging to Messy Church countries, find the country on the map and, with a blob of Blu Tack, fix the flag to the map.

Talk about the fact that there are Messy Churches all over the world sharing the good news of Jesus! They have all started thanks to the faithful work of Messy Church disciples being led by God, spreading the good news and praying for people everywhere. See how many Messy Churches you can find. Take time to pray for them.

Session material: June

7. Concertina paper people

You will need: A4 paper; a dinner plate about 20 cm in diameter; pencil; pens; scissors; coloured card; glue

Trace around the plate and cut out a circle of paper. Fold it in half three times. With the paper still folded, draw half of a person on the left side (on the fold) and half on the right side (on the fold), with their hands holding in the middle of the paper. Cut out and open your circle of people. Stick on to coloured card and decorate.

Talk about how the circle of people reminds us of the importance of being together with other Christians, so we can grow strong in our faith and learn to be disciples of God.

8. Galaxy dough creations

You will need: galaxy play dough; star cutters; card in different colours; star-shaped paper plates; string; hole punch

Make your galaxy play-dough by adding blue and red food colouring to make a deep space colour. Add coloured glitter to form a galaxy of stars.

Press the dough in to the star-shaped plates. Using the star cutters, make some stars from the card. Add some stars to your plate by pressing them into the dough. Punch a hole in the plate and hang with the string.

Talk about how big the galaxy and the world are. God thought of everything and created stars to light up the sky. He created us to be dazzling disciples, spreading God's light to all the world.

9. Dancing disciples

You will need: balloons (dazzling colours, if possible); thin tissue paper; scissors; felt-tip pens; sticky tape

Draw a picture of a disciple on the tissue paper, and carefully colour with felt-tip pens. Cut out your disciple. If the tissue is two-ply, then pull the plys apart. Tape the disciple's feet to the table. Blow up your balloon and knot it. Rub the balloon through your hair or woollen jersey for about 10–20 seconds and see if you can make your disciple stand up and dance!

Talk about what you think helped make the tissue disciples get up and dance. How does God help us to be his disciples?

10. Dazzling disciple dress-ups

You will need: dazzling clothes; paper; crêpe paper; string; fabric scraps; glue; glitter

Make hats, headbands, scarfs or accessories and dress up to look like a dazzling disciple.

Talk about how we can make our lives shine the love of Jesus.

6

7

8

9

10

Dazzling disciples by Jocelyn Czerwonka

Celebration

What did you discover about being a disciple from the Acrostic Disciple challenge? What interesting words, alliterations or sentences did you all come up with? For example, we came up with: Dazzling disciples dutifully dedicated to God. Have you ever thought of yourself as a dazzling disciple?

Do you ever look up into the stars and think about what an amazing God we have to make stars so bright?

What is so amazing about stars? (*Ask some people to give you suggestions.*) They dazzle and twinkle in the dark night; they give light to the dark; they help people to find their way, just like the wise men searching for baby Jesus. A long time ago, long before Jesus was born, God said to Abram: 'Look at the sky and try to count the stars; you will have as many descendants as that' (Genesis 15:5, GNT). Even though Abram and his wife Sarai were old, God promised them as many children, great-grandchildren, great-great-great-great grandchildren as the stars in the sky. And God wants all of those children to be his disciples – people who are followers of God. That means we have some work to do!

Can you dazzle like a star? I'm sure as one of God's children you can – whatever your age! Think about how you can be a dazzling disciple, showing love and care to your family, friends and neighbours. Sometimes, to be a dazzling disciple, it's not about what you say, but what you do, how you behave, how you show kindness and love to others. Can you shine bright like a star so people can see God's love shining from you?

In the Bible, it talks about the new believers meeting together daily, learning, eating, praying and praising God together (Acts 2:42-47) – a bit like we do at Messy Church. Maybe you can think of people who would like to become new believers and invite them to Messy Church next time. Let's take time to pray together for places and people all over the world.

Prayer

You will need: a brightly coloured ball of wool for each group – dazzling colours would be great

Everyone stand in a circle (up to 12–15 people per circle). The first person holds tightly to one end of a ball of wool, calls out their own name and then a person (first name), country, town, village, school, Messy Church or place they would like included in the prayers. They then throw the ball to another person across the circle and they also call out their name and another person or place. This is repeated around the circle as many times as you like, but remember everyone needs to hold tight to the wool. By the end, everyone should have had a turn and there will be a criss-crossing of wool and prayers around the world.

Discipleship happens when we all work together as a team, like the wool that has come together to form something beautiful. The leader or a volunteer can pray for all the people or places named and ask God to help us all be dazzling disciples, wherever we go.

Song suggestions

'I've got the joy, joy, joy down in my heart' – Heritage Kids
'This little light of mine' – traditional/public domain
'Go tell everyone' – John J. DiModica
'There were twelve disciples' – traditional

Meal suggestion

Corn Chips with mince and/or vegetarian option of black beans in a tomato sauce, dazzled with grated cheese. Add corn kernels for a star effect.

For dessert, serve blackcurrant jelly with yellow jelly stars. (For stars, make a firm white jelly using half the amount of water required and a little coconut milk to whiten. Allow to set. Pour over a firm yellow jelly, also using half the amount of water required. When set, cut into star shapes and place on to the blackcurrant jelly.) Serve with fruit and ice cream.

Session material: July

Holy Habit: Worship

 Go to messychurch.org.uk/
getmessymay19 to download all
templates at A4 size, including a
session planning sheet

#discipleship: individual

Messy reflection by Martyn Payne

Lord, our Lord, how majestic is your name in the
wholeearth!

You have set your glory in the heavens. You have
made sure that children and infants praise you. Their
praise is a wall that stops the talk of your enemies.

I think about the heavens. I think about what your
fingers have created. I think about the moon and stars
that you have set in place. What are human beings that
you think about them? What is a son of man that you take
care of him? You have made them a little lower than the
angels. You placed on them a crown of glory and honour.

You made human beings rule over everything your
hands created. You put everything under their control.
They rule over all flocks and herds and over the wild
animals. They rule over the birds in the sky and over the
fish in the ocean. They rule over everything that swims
in the oceans.

Lord, our Lord, how majestic is your name in the
whole earth!

Psalm 8 (NIRV)

The book of Psalms is an amazing collection of poems,
prayers and songs of praise. They give us words for all sorts
of occasions and moods in the messy rough and tumble of
everyday life. Some of your Messy Church congregation may
be surprised to discover that, as well as expressing thanks
and delight in God, it is also okay to argue with God, express
despair and depression, shout angrily about things that are
wrong and even have doubts about God's love. All this is in the
Psalms – and a lot more. It is an important resource.

Psalm 8 is a great outburst of praise and wonder, inspired by
looking up into a night sky that is bright with stars. We too
are awed by the majesty of the heavens and prompted to ask
the big questions such as, 'Is there a God?', and if there is,
'What is God like?', and then, significantly, 'What part do I play
in all this?' The stars, galaxies and solar systems above bear
witness to God's grandeur. The power of God is made visible

by glimpsing the immensity of the universe. And the psalmist
concludes that human beings are a special part of this glory,
each with a unique job to do, ruling it on God's behalf. God is
the star-maker and God makes people – you and me – 'star
attractions' within that creation.

For many of us, it was in childhood that faith was nurtured
as we encountered the wonder of the heavens. Perhaps this
is why David includes the verse about the praises of children.
It might even be that this is a psalm from David's own early
years, composed while he was out in the fields, watching over
the sheep beneath a starlit night sky.

#discipleship: team

Messy health check

Go round the team and each say what it is about Jesus that
excites you most at this point in your life. Pray about this.

Messy team theme

- How do you encourage one another to worship God?
- Can you identify worship in all the parts of Messy Church?
- How can you help others see God is worthy of our praise?

How does this session help people grow in Christ?

This psalm encourages us to praise God and see that we are
not alone in praising him. We are reminded of the worth and
majesty and greatness of God, the God who loves and cares
for each one of us. We are reminded that all of creation praises
God, that all things are made by God and that God has given a
special job to humans – the care of all of his creation. We are
encouraged by the might and majesty of God and the result is
that we praise him in and through our worship of him.

#discipleship: families

Mealtime card

- How do you like to worship God?
- What is your favourite song to praise God?
- Where is the most unusual place you have worshipped?
- What do you do to show people you think they are fab?

Take-home idea

When it gets dark, look up and see if you can see the stars. Find
out about the different stars and see if you can identify any.
Have a quiet moment and think about God making the stars in

Everything worships God by Anne Offler and Sharon Pritchard

the sky and then remember that God made you and all of your family. Think of a good praise sentence to say to God.

Question to start and end the session

So… how does creation worship God?

#discipleship: extra

Have a 'Starty' (a Star Party) and get together to stargaze. Read Psalm 8 as part of your evening.

Social action

In the book of Micah, God's people are asked to worship God first of all by 'acting justly'. Challenge each other to do one thing this month to bring justice to your world.

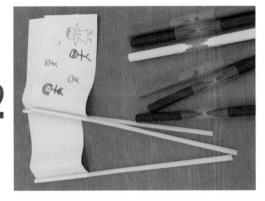

Activities

1. Majestic name

You will need: air-dry clay; beads; sequins; laminated sheets of A4 coloured card or paper

Roll a piece of clay into a long sausage shape. Use the clay to make the individual letters of the word 'God' and put them on to one of the coloured laminated boards. Push beads and sequins into the clay word to decorate it. Take it home and let it dry.

Talk about God's name and how it is described as majestic. What does majestic mean? Do you think this is a good description of God?

2. Praise flags

You will need: card flag shapes (available from Baker Ross) or card rectangles; drinking straws; sticky tape; felt-tip pens

Draw lots of members of your family and your friends on a flag using the coloured pens. Attach the stick to the card to finish the flag.

Talk about all the earth praising God. How do you praise God? Can you wave the flag and make a noise? Be ready to take your flag to the celebration to praise God with everyone else.

3. Fish and birds suncatcher

You will need: laminating pouches; laminator; scraps of tissue paper; coloured cling film (cellophane); silver or gold foil stars; scissors; hole punch; ribbon; large bird or fish shapes; marker pens

Fill a laminating pouch with scraps of tissue paper, coloured cling film and little silver or gold foil stars. Work with an adult to put the pouch through the laminator. Place the bird or fish template on to the pouch, draw round it with the marker pen and cut out the shape. Add ribbon and hang in the window.

Talk about the different fish and birds God has made – so many colours and shapes and sizes! They are all beautiful and special. We are all different, too. In what ways are we different from birds and fish and from one another? Do you think we are beautiful and special?

Additional copies can be purchased at **brfonline.org.uk/9780857467751** or using the order form on page 39.

Session material: July

4. He's got the whole world in his hands

You will need: thick card; large circular picture of the world from where you are; coloured paper; pencils; marker pens; scissors; glue

Stick the picture of the world on to the thick card and cut around the edge to make a circle. Draw round your hands on coloured paper and cut them out. Stick one hand on each side of the bottom of the world you have just made, as if the hands are holding it. Write the words 'He's got the whole world in his hands' across the world or the hands.

Talk about what it might mean that God holds the world in his hands. How do we know that God cares?

5. Animal runaround bingo

You will need: a master sheet of twelve animal black-and-white outlines; photocopies of this sheet (one for each child or family); twelve smaller pieces of paper with one of the animals on each (each animal coloured something different); sticky tack; coloured pencils or pens

Preparation: Stick or place the coloured clue cards around the room. Put the pens or pencils on a central table.

Each child or family should have a sheet of uncoloured animals. Go around the room until one of the clue cards is found. Look at it, leave it where it is and return to the central table and colour the animal on your sheet to match. Continue until all of the animals have been found and your sheet is completely coloured.

Talk about all of the animals God made. Which one is your favourite? How many can you name?

6. Worship at God's throne

You will need: a high-backed chair; coloured fabric; a crown; large pieces of paper or card with the outlines of words 'WORSHIP', 'GOD' or 'HOLY'; small coloured pebbles

Make a throne using the coloured fabric. Place the words in front of the throne. Take a pebble and hold it. Think about God or pray to him quietly before placing it on one of the words. Add as many stones as you would like to.

Talk about worshipping God before his throne as something special to do.

🇫 📷 🐦 **@MessyChurchBRF**

Additional copies can be purchased at **brfonline.org.uk/9780857467751** or using the order form on page 39.

Everything worships God by Anne Offler and Sharon Pritchard

7. The night sky

You will need: star and moon cookie cutters; plates; slices of bread; assorted sandwich fillings; knives (not sharp)

Make a sandwich using the filling items provided. Using the cookie cutters, cut out shapes from the sandwich and make a night sky. Put your cut sandwiches on your plate for later.

Talk about how the night sky is lit up by the stars and the moon. Have you seen the moon? Have you seen the stars? Do you think we will be able to see them tonight?

8. Amazing angels

You will need: chenille wires (pipe cleaners); ribbon

Make a loop in the middle of one of the wires. Join the ends of the wire by twisting them flat and form into a triangle for the body. With the other wire, twist two loops for the wings, leaving a few centimetres at each end. Lay the head and body part on the wings and twist the ends of the wings around each side of the body. Attach the ribbon to hang up the angel.

Talk about angels being very special to God. How/why do you think they are special? People are nearly as special as angels. Do you think that makes people special?

9. Worship words

You will need: a Scrabble board and letters

Use the letters to make words used to worship God. Build them up on the board, overlapping them as you do when you play Scrabble.

Talk about the words you have made. Look at the words made by others. Which words do you think you would use to worship God?

10. Egg-box animals

You will need: egg cartons with each egg cup cut out; pens; scissors; chenille wires (pipe cleaners); glue; googly eyes; paint; paint brushes; scraps of felt, fabric, etc.

Make a range of animals using egg cups. Paint or colour the cut-up egg box, using the materials on the table to make the animals.

Talk about the animals God made and how we look after them, protect them, value them.

Session material: July
Everything worships God
by Anne Offler and Sharon Pritchard

Celebration

I wonder how you tell people that you think they are fab, that they are kind, that you love them? I wonder how you would show this? (*Take some examples and all practise together.*)

A man called David, who lived years and years ago, wanted to tell God that he was fab, that he was kind and that he loved him, so he wrote a song. He actually wrote lots of songs and some of them are in the Bible in a book called Psalms. We have been looking at one of the psalms today, Psalm 8. In this song, David is telling God that he is the greatest. And David says that everything worships God.

Split the group into five small groups. Give each group the following actions:

- Group one: Wave flags or your arms
- Group two: Flick your fingers out like stars, hold your hands in a moon shape or draw a sun in the air
- Group three: Choose an animal and do actions of that animal
- Group four: Choose a bird and do actions of that bird
- Group five: Choose something that swims in the sea and do that action

Count to three and have everyone do their action together, then stop.

Get ready to read the psalm and ask everyone to listen carefully and, at your prompt, do their action. Stop when the next group starts.

All start by saying together, 'Lord, our Lord, how majestic is your name in all the earth!' (NIRV). As you read verses 1b–2, have the first group wave their flags or their arms. Read verses 3–5 and have the second group do stars, sun and moon shapes. Read verses 6–7 with group three doing their animal actions. Read verse 8 and have groups four and five together do their bird or fish action. Invite everyone to say the last verse together doing their group actions: 'Lord, our Lord, how majestic is your name in all the earth!' (After you have read this through once, you might want to repeat it as people now know what they are doing!)

So, everything worships God and so do we. Let's get ready to do some more worship as we sing, wave flags, pray and go about our lives every day.

Prayer

(Use the five groups who will do their actions as their action is mentioned.)

Loving Lord God, we worship you. Children and grown-ups worship you (*group one*), the sun and moon and stars worship you (*group two*), animals (*group three*) and birds (*group four*) and fish (*group five*) all worship you and *we* worship you. We say a huge thank you for loving us and caring for us. We think you are amazing for making the world and everything in it. We think you are so fab and we want to tell you how much we love you, so we say: 'We love you, Lord' (*all wave flags or hands*). Amen

Song suggestions

'He's got the whole world in his hands' – traditional
'Hosanna, hosanna, hosanna in the highest' – Carl Tuttle
'We praise God' – Alan Price

Meal suggestion

Assorted food buffet – sandwiches from the activity, crisps or chips, salad or vegetables. For dessert, have creamy rice pudding and fruit e.g. peaches.

Session material: August
Created for community by Lindsey Goodyear

Holy Habit: Fellowship

 Go to **messychurch.org.uk/ getmessymay19** to download all templates at A4 size, including a session planning sheet

#discipleship: individual

Messy reflection by Jocelyn Czerwonka

This is the account of the heavens and the earth when they were created, when the Lord God made the earth and the heavens.

Now no shrub had yet appeared on the earth and no plant had yet sprung up, for the Lord God had not sent rain on the earth and there was no one to work the ground, but streams came up from the earth and watered the whole surface of the ground. Then the Lord God formed a man from the dust of the ground and breathed into his nostrils the breath of life, and the man became a living being…

The Lord God said, 'It is not good for the man to be alone. I will make a helper suitable for him.'

Now the Lord God had formed out of the ground all the wild animals and all the birds in the sky. He brought them to the man to see what he would name them; and whatever the man called each living creature, that was its name. So the man gave names to all the livestock, the birds in the sky and all the wild animals.

But for Adam no suitable helper was found. So the Lord God caused the man to fall into a deep sleep; and while he was sleeping, he took one of the man's ribs and then closed up the place with flesh. Then the Lord God made a woman from the rib he had taken out of the man, and he brought her to the man.

Genesis 2:4–7, 18–22 (NIV)

God had a good idea: 'I'm going to make something!' But what? It needed to be big, beautiful, fun and free. So it was that God created our beautiful universe and world with its teeming life, colour, wet and dry, light and darkness, and freedom. And God also created people, not just one on his own (Adam) but two (Eve, as well) and then more and more and more – until we came along! More will follow until all is ready for God to complete the grand design of life and join us for a big party.

The story of creation in Genesis is likely very familiar, but don't let that stop us from noticing its special features. First, God chose to create; nothing forced God's hand. Next, even the heavenly bodies – the sun, moon and stars – were made by God. God took time and care about this process. The seven days describe a process of unfolding development. They also include a period of rest, a repeating sequence that still forms the pattern of family and communal life.

The animals named by Adam were potential companions but not quite right as equals. Some animals were tamed to become domestic, while even the wild creatures had their purpose and place. But God formed the woman out of the same flesh as the man. Adam and Eve were of equal origin so could have a relationship of mutuality, which was not possible with the animals. God intends us to live in companionship, but with another voice and opinion comes the possibility of making choices against God's will. We likely know the second part of the creation story: at the advice of the serpent, Adam and Eve were tempted and fell into sin by listening to someone other than God. They chose to redefine good and evil according to their own desires. Making choices, for good or evil, is part of the reality of living in community.

#discipleship: team

Messy health check

If your team was a toolkit, what item would each person be?

Messy team theme

- How has the fellowship you've developed within your Messy team helped your own personal growth?
- How has God specifically had a hand in that growth?
- How do we help support that same growth in our Messy Church members?

How does this session help people grow in Christ?

When God created the heavens and the earth, there was an expectation he had from humanity: do not eat from the tree in the middle of the garden. Though he knew what would happen, God watched as Adam and Eve listened to the manipulations of the serpent instead of his own word. Because of this, the original sin, our world was changed from the perfection that was the garden of Eden to a world that knows suffering. Thankfully, there is still a light at the end of our tunnel.

Additional copies can be purchased at **brfonline.org.uk/9780857467751** or using the order form on page 39.

Session material: August

Through the forgiveness of God and the blood Christ shed for us, we can all know eternal salvation. We must work together, here on earth, for a companionship with Christ that we can call fellowship. The importance of building a loving and abiding group foundation that will hold us accountable and help us grow in his word is imperative to a successful walk with God.

#discipleship: families

Mealtime card

- When God created the world, he expected fellowship from his people. What do you think life would have been like for us if Adam and Eve had not given in to the temptation of the serpent?
- What is your favourite part of the fellowship you've found at Messy Church?
- How do you think praying for each other can strengthen fellowship in a church?

Take-home idea

Choose one verse a week to study with your family at home. Each day, set aside 10–15 minutes to discuss individual thoughts on the verse. One of the most beautiful things about studying the Bible is that you get different perspectives from your brothers and sisters in Christ. Work as hard to build fellowship in the home as you do at your church.

Dear heavenly Father, we ask that you continue to show us love and grace through our imperfections. We ask that you help us to find the good in each other so we can live in this world you so lovingly created for us with a feeling of encouragement from those around us. Help us to continue to build our love for you through a Christ-centred community and give us the words to inspire those who have not yet found you to start looking. Amen

Question to start and end the session

So… what does fellowship mean to you?

#discipleship: extra

Do something for the isolated people in your local community: who are they? What would be ideal?

Social action

Collect ideas on a display board of all the ways your community falls short of God's perfect way of living. Talk about what you could do together to change things for the better.

1

2

3

4

🅵 📌 🆇 **@MessyChurchBRF**

Created for community by Lindsey Goodyear

Activities

1. Fellowship cloud

You will need: a large roll of paper; coloured ribbon; glue; paper; scissors; markers

Work as a group to cut a large cloud out of a large roll of paper. Attach different-length ribbons to hang from the bottom of it. In the centre of the cloud, write Galatians 3:26: 'So in Christ Jesus you are all children of God through faith' (NIV). Decorate your own name tag to attach to some part of a hanging ribbon to show that we are all children of God.

Talk about how uniquely and perfectly each one of us is made in God's image.

2. Praying fizz

You will need: fizzy vitamin tablets; water; a glass

Give each person a fizzy vitamin tablet and set a glass of water in the middle of the table. Have the activity volunteer explain how excited God gets when we work on developing our fellowship through prayer, gatherings and supporting one another through Christ. Allow the vitamin to represent our fellowship and the glass of water to represent God. Have them drop their tablet into the water and watch the 'excitement' that 'God' (the water) shows when we work together to follow his word.

Talk about a time when you felt excited during worship.

3. Take-home prayer

You will need: paper, pens/pencils, and a bucket

Part of fellowship means praying for others, not just yourself. Write down one or two personal prayer requests, then drop the paper into a bucket and mix it up. Before the end of the night, each person should take a piece of paper from the bucket to bring home and thoughtfully pray for others from Messy Church.

Talk about a situation you prayed for that was answered in God's perfect timing.

4. Faith identity bracelets

You will need: empty paper towel rolls cut into three-inch long tubes; scissors; felt-tip pens; stickers; paint; paint brushes

Take the empty paper towel roll and cut down the long side. This will create a cuff that will fit around your wrist. Write 'child of God' on the outside and decorate the rest with stickers, pens or paint.

Talk about what it means to be brothers and sisters in Christ. What are the advantages to such close fellowship?

5. Walking on eggs

You will need: four to eight boxes of a dozen eggs

With all the eggs still inside their boxes, ask people what they think would happen if you were to put your full weight on the eggs (most will say they'd break). Allow one person after another to walk across the top of the egg containers and see that they stay perfectly intact. Explain that the experiment is exactly the same as our walk with God. When we put our faith in him, the seemingly impossible becomes possible.

Talk about a time where the seemingly impossible was made possible by giving your doubts to God.

6. The fellowship fire

You will need: white paper or card; brown paper; yellow and orange tissue paper; glue; scissors; pens

Take a piece of white paper or card. Using yellow and orange tissue paper, create a fire and glue it to the paper/card. Cut out a number of small rectangles from brown paper (the fire logs) and write one word or phrase on each log of what fellowship means to them. Glue the logs on to the paper as well, under the fire.

Talk about how to keep the fire of fellowship alive. How can we be sure not to let our fire for the Lord fizzle out?

7. Walking colours

You will need: six glass jars; water; food colouring; paper towels

A huge part of fellowship is what our walk with God looks like. Using the food colouring, fill the six glass jars with different coloured water and set them close together in a row. Take a paper towel and put one end in the first jar and the other end in the second, then again with the second and third, and so on. Watch as the water 'walks' from one jar to the next and the colours combine.

Talk about how the flow of our lives looks different in fellowship than it does on our own, like the colours flowing together in this activity.

Session material: August

8. Walk with Jesus

You will need: a large roll of paper; flat pans; colourful paint

Create a line from one end of the room to the other using a large roll of paper. Barefooted, take turns stepping into flat pans of coloured paint and walking across the length of the paper. At the end of the meeting, have fun observing all the different colours and sizes of prints. Explain that even though we may all be different, the road we're taking is the same.

Talk about walking together with the Lord. How can we hold each other accountable to stay on the right path?

9. Raise your hand

You will need: a large piece of paper; decorative paper; pens; scissors; glue; felt-tip pens

Hang a large rectangular-shaped piece of paper on the wall with the words, 'Raise your hand if you're a child of God' written across the middle. Have members outline, cut out and individually decorate (optional) their own hand prints (up to about mid forearm). Glue the cutouts around the outside of the large paper and enjoy the colourful art they've created!

Talk about how our world might have been different if Adam and Eve had raised their hands as a child of God instead of giving into temptation.

10. Strong foundation Jenga

You will need: several games of Jenga; sticky tape; felt-tip pens

Take a little wooden block and write words or phrases that represent fellowship to you (you can cover one side with a piece of tape and write on that if you don't want the ink on the actual wood pieces). Stack the blocks the same way you would in the game (three one way, three the other). Explain that fellowship means following all aspects of God's word and if we start abandoning bits and pieces here and there, the foundation of our faith will crumble. Play your Jenga game, taking out the blocks piece by piece and see how long before the tower crumbles.

Talk about how having a strong foundation with Christ can strengthen the fellowship you have with others.

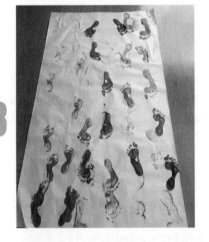

Created for community by Lindsey Goodyear

Celebration

In the very first garden, God instructed Adam and Eve, the very first humans, to stay away from the tree that was forbidden. However, after some bad influence from the serpent, the two of them gave in, thus changing the world we live in with sin. In reality, we will all deal with our own versions of the 'serpent' every day. Pressures and temptations to do what we would like, instead of following God's word, are all around us. For example, standing up to peer pressure can be nearly impossible. Though it may be hard, we have to stay strong in our faith and follow what our heavenly Father asks of us. There is a reason they call it 'the road less travelled'! If it were easy, everyone would be walking it perfectly. Keep God's word nearby and do your best to separate yourselves from the 'serpents' of the world.

Divide the congregation into small groups (maybe five or so). Give each group ten water bottles and one rubber ball. Nine of the water bottles should be full and one should be empty. Have the group experiment with different ways of setting up the bottles and hurling the ball toward them. They must figure out a way to knock over all of the full bottles and leave the empty one standing. At the end of the experiment, have the groups explain which formation worked best for them. Ultimately, for the empty water bottle to remain standing, it is best to keep it as far away as possible from the others.

Explain that the full water bottles represent the things in life which God loves us to enjoy. These are things that will 'fill' our lives with goodness but may be harder to knock over, just like staying on the road of righteousness is a difficult task. The empty bottle represents something that would disappoint God. These decisions bring us 'emptiness' in life. The empty water is easier to knock over and, like sometimes in life, this road seems easier to take than the road less travelled. The further we keep away from the things that bring God sadness, the more we will please him.

Prayer

Since a huge part of fellowship is working together and supporting one another, invite a small group of members up to do a multipart prayer, each person thanking God for something relating to Messy Church. Have one member start and, before they finish, let another join in by saying their thanksgiving, and so on and so on. All will say 'Amen' when the last person has finished.

Song suggestions

'Blessed assurance' – Third Day
'We're on this road' – Fischy Music
'I am loved' – Heather Price
'In the sweet by and by' – Ben Hester
'How great thou art' – Lauren Daigle

Meal suggestion

Pizza with every topping (save some with no meat as a vegetarian option) to represent all of us together in fellowship. Sides can include seasonal fruit or salad.

Give each person a dry cupcake and set out a bowl of frosting, sprinkles and other edible decorations to let them decorate their own desserts.

Dear Jane

Advice for Messy Church leaders from Jane Leadbetter

✉ Email **jane.leadbetter@brf.org.uk** with your Messy questions and for advice.

Phil in Leicester

How do we go about getting food hygiene certificates for our Messy Church team? We are already so busy and give a lot of time in preparation and delivery. How many hours are the courses for?

Hi Phil

There are various companies that offer online courses. If you look on the internet, you will find courses at a reasonable rate which, on average, take about three hours to complete. Some courses you can complete a section at a time. Messy Churches have recommended the following as a starter for you: **virtual-college. co.uk/courses/food-hygiene-courses/level-2-food-hygiene-for-catering** and **thesaferfoodgroup.com**.

Level 2 options seem to be the most popular and include food preparation, handling, storage and serving. You can print off your certificate at the end of the course. There is a handy checklist for hygiene requirements at: **food.gov.uk/business-guidance/hygiene-requirements-for-your-business**.

Joanne in Yorkshire

We would like to attach a Messy Church banner to some railings near our church. Would we need permission? Who from?

Hi Joanne

Please contact your local council for information. Some councils give permission so long as the banner is not permanent; some councils say between 14 to 30 days is okay. It may also depend on whether you are in a conservation area. Examples of Messy Church banners can be found at CPO (Christian Publishing & Outreach), who supply lots of Messy Church merchandise: **cpo.org.uk**. There are new free digital visuals to use, too.

Sharon in Cheshire

I was recently in my local Christian bookshop looking for resources to give to my Messy Church baptism families. The bookshop could not suggest anything, which disappointed me. Do you have any ideas?

Hi Sharon

We are finding that the Messy Church minibooks range is proving rather popular as gifts for Messy families. Many Messy Churches have been asking for something like this. We can now offer interactive, user-friendly and jargon-free booklets designed to help families talk about the basics of the Christian faith. *Family Question Time* (just £2.50) is one option, with a discount available on multiple copies. Find these minibooks at **brfonline.org.uk**.

Andrew in Surrey

My Messy Church planning team comprises myself, my vicar, a lay person and a young leader who can only come intermittently. How can I help them to focus on the vision and discipleship opportunities that Messy Church can give to this parish? I am struggling to communicate the importance of this mission in our community.

Hi Andrew

We applaud your endeavour! Have you seen our Messy Church Discipleship Pilot or the Messy Church Self-Review Toolkit? These tools could help you to choose a Messy Church value each time your planning team meets. They encourage you to explore your Messy Church and revisit your aims and objectives and explore avenues of opportunity. Get out the coffee and cake, and pick which approach you will take. Lots of downloadable documents are on our Messy Church website at **messychurch.org.uk/discipleship**. Some Messy Church teams are choosing a Messy Extra, or focusing more on prayer. Other avenues could be mentoring a family or engaging in some social action. Get excited about the Messy opportunities! Please feed back to us anything that you try.

Order your next issue of *Get Messy!*

Get Messy! is published three times per year in January, May and September.
Available from: your local Christian bookshop   By phone: +44 (0)1865 319700
Online: brfonline.org.uk/getmessy   By post: complete the form below

Print copies

SUBSCRIPTION (INCLUDES POSTAGE AND PACKING)	PRICE	QTY	TOTAL (£)
September 2019 to August 2020 one-year subscription (UK)	£17.40		
September 2019 to August 2020 one-year subscription (Europe)	£25.50		
September 2019 to August 2020 one-year subscription (Rest of world)	£29.40		
SINGLE COPIES	PRICE	QTY	TOTAL (£)
Get Messy! May–August 2019	£4.60		
Get Messy! September–December 2019	£4.60		
Postage for single copies (see right)			
Donation to BRF's Messy Church			
		Total	

Title .... First name/initials .... Surname ....

Address ....

.... Postcode ....

Telephone .... Email ....

Method of payment

☐ Cheque (made payable to BRF)   ☐ MasterCard / Visa

Card no. ☐☐☐☐ ☐☐☐☐ ☐☐☐☐ ☐☐☐☐ ☐☐☐☐

Valid from ☐☐ ☐☐   Expires ☐☐ ☐☐   Security code* ☐☐☐
                                        Last 3 digits on the reverse of the card

Signature .... Date ....
ESSENTIAL IN ORDER TO PROCESS YOUR ORDER

Messy Church is part of BRF, a Registered Charity (233280)

A **group subscription** works when you receive five or more copies of *Get Messy!* delivered to a single address. To order postage-free, go to brfonline.org. uk/getmessy#Groupsubscriptions.

BRF

Digital copies

Single-copy purchases of the *Get Messy!* magazine are intended for the sole use of the purchaser. If you would like to distribute digital copies to your Messy Church team, simply click the **Buy now** button on the product page and add the number of copies you need into the quantity box. The following discounts will be applied for multiple copies:

1–2 copies: no discount   3–4 copies: 10% discount
5–9 copies: 15% discount   10+ copies: 20% discount

For further information about purchasing digital copies and copyright information, see **brfonline.org.uk/terms**.

POSTAGE AND PACKING CHARGES			
Order value	UK	Europe	Rest of world
Under £7.00	£2.00	£5.00	£7.00
£7.00–£29.99	£3.00	£9.00	£15.00
£30.00+	FREE	£9.00 + 15% of order value	£15.00 + 20% of order value

General information

Delivery times within the UK are normally 15 working days. All prices are subject to the current rate of VAT. Prices are correct at the time of going to press but may change without prior notice. Offers available while stocks last.

Return this form with the appropriate payment to:

BRF, 15 The Chambers, Vineyard, Abingdon OX14 3FE
Tel. +44 (0)1865 319700   Fax +44 (0)1865 319701

To read our terms and find out about cancelling your order, please visit **brfonline.org.uk/terms**.

You can pay for your annual subscription using Direct Debit. You need only give your bank details once, and the payment is made automatically every year until you cancel it. If you would like to pay by Direct Debit, please also use the form below, entering your BRF account number under 'Reference' if you know it. You are fully covered by the Direct Debit Guarantee.

Instruction to your bank or building society to pay by Direct Debit

Please fill in the whole form using a ballpoint pen and return it to:
BRF, 15 The Chambers, Vineyard, Abingdon OX14 3FE

Service User Number: 5 5 8 2 2 9

Name and full postal address of your bank or building society

To: The Manager .... Bank/Building Society

Address ....

....

Postcode ....

☐☐☐☐☐☐☐☐

Instruction to your Bank/Building Society
Please pay The Bible Reading Fellowship Direct Debits from the account detailed in this instruction, subject to the safeguards assured by the Direct Debit Guarantee. I understand that this instruction may remain with The Bible Reading Fellowship and, if so, details will be passed electronically to my bank/building society.

Signature(s)

Name(s) of account holder(s)

Branch sort code   Bank/Building Society account number
☐☐–☐☐–☐☐   ☐☐☐☐☐☐☐☐

Reference number

Banks and Building Societies may not accept Direct Debit instructions for some types of account.

The Direct Debit Guarantee

- This Guarantee is offered by all banks and building societies that accept instructions to pay Direct Debits.
- If there are any changes to the amount, date or frequency of your Direct Debit, The Bible Reading Fellowship will notify you 10 working days in advance of your account being debited or as otherwise agreed. If you request The Bible Reading Fellowship to collect a payment, confirmation of the amount and date will be given to you at the time of the request.
- If an error is made in the payment of your Direct Debit, by The Bible Reading Fellowship or your bank or building society, you are entitled to a full and immediate refund of the amount paid from your bank or building society.
- If you receive a refund you are not entitled to, you must pay it back when The Bible Reading Fellowship asks you to.
- You can cancel a Direct Debit at any time by simply contacting your bank or building society. Written confirmation may be required. Please also notify us.

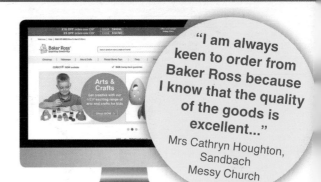

getMESSY!

One holy,
catholic and
apostolic
church

Messy
weddings

Bible overview,
part 2

Survey
results
are in!

BRF, 15 The Chambers, Vineyard, Abingdon OX14 3FE
+44 (0)1865 319700 | enquiries@brf.org.uk
brf.org.uk

Messy Church is part of The Bible Reading Fellowship,
a Registered Charity (233280)

ISBN 978 0 85746 612 9
First published 2018
10 9 8 7 6 5 4 3 2 1 0
All rights reserved

This edition © The Bible Reading Fellowship 2018

Acknowledgements

Scripture quotations taken from *The Message*,
copyright © 1993, 1994, 1995, 1996, 2000, 2001,
2002 by Eugene H. Peterson. Used by permission
of NavPress. All rights reserved. Represented by
Tyndale House Publishers, Inc.

Scripture quotations taken from the Holy Bible,
New Living Translation, copyright © 1996, 2004,
2007, 2013. Used by permission of Tyndale House
Publishers, Inc., Carol Stream, Illinois 60188. All
rights reserved.

Scripture quotations taken from The Holy Bible, New
International Version (Anglicised edition), copyright
© 1979, 1984, 2011 by Biblica. Used by permission
of Hodder & Stoughton Publishers, a Hachette UK
company. All rights reserved. 'NIV' is a registered
trademark of Biblica. UK trademark number
1448790.

Scripture quotations from the Good News Bible,
published by The Bible Societies/HarperCollins
Publishers Ltd, UK © American Bible Society 1966,
1971, 1976, 1992, used with permission.

Editor: Olivia Warburton
Subeditor: Rachel Tranter
Proofreader: Kathryn Glendenning
Designer: Rebecca J Hall
Cover photo: Lesley Cox

Printed in the UK by Stephens & George Print Group

Note for subscribers

Print copies are dispatched to arrive six weeks
prior to the date on the cover of the magazine.
The May 2019 issue should be with you around
the middle of March 2019. The PDF version of
the magazine is also available for purchase and
immediate download from the beginning of March.
messychurch.org.uk/resources/get-messy

Photocopying for churches

To order back issues of *Get Messy!* and other Messy
Church resources, email BRF at **enquiries@brf.org.uk**
or telephone **+44 (0)1865 319700**.

Send in news, stories, photos and general enquiries
to our Messy Church administrator on **+44 (0)1235
858238** or **messychurch@brf.org.uk**.

Meet our session writers for this issue

Becky May lives with her husband and two young
children in Bedfordshire, where she is Messy Church
Regional Coordinator. Becky is co-founder of The
Treasure Box People and is very much at home with
all things messy!

Jean Pienaar lives in Johannesburg, South Africa.
She started a Messy Church in 2009 and is now one of
the Messy Church Regional Coordinators. She enjoys
a busy, messy life within the demands of traffic,
laundry, regular meals and family, and tries to find
holy moments and sacred beauty in the chaos.

Jen Robertson is the Children's Resources Manager
of the Scottish Bible Society. Part of her remit is to
help all generations engage with the Bible together.
She is part of Burnside Blairbeth Messy Church
in Rutherglen near Glasgow, which she helped to
launch. She loves to run and read but not necessarily
at the same time!

Greg Ross is a Uniting Church minister in Bunbury in
the south of Western Australia. He is the Messy Church
Regional Coordinator for Western Australia and is part
of the National Messy Team for Australia. Greg and his
family all play their part in their local Messy Church,
which was the second one to start in Australia.

Themes in this edition

Over the next four months of sessions in this magazine, we'll
be exploring four aspects of Jesus bringing life in all its fullness
to people of all ages. We'll be encouraging everyone to think
about Jesus' sense of belonging to his heavenly Father and
what that means for our sense of belonging (**January**); our self-
confidence, as God has a job for each of us, just as he had for
the unlikely Gideon (**February**); the unconditional forgiveness
we can receive from Jesus and can give to others as we look
at the story of the woman forgiven by Jesus (**March**); and the
rock-solid hope and trust that Jesus is always with us that comes
from the Easter story (**April**).

Over these last twelve months in the magazine, we've been
responding to the deepest fears and needs expressed by
children and young people in the UK, as highlighted in the Good
Childhood Report. As we welcome new families and individuals
to our church family, we are both fellow children of God and
responsible parents in that family. In our Messy Churches, we
are enjoying rediscovering the joys of belonging to this family
as children ourselves and trying to love wisely, as generous
parents. Together with family members new and old, younger
and older, we explore facets of our faith that bring us closer to
the life Jesus longs for us to enjoy.

1. Ask God to bless and guide you as you consider what's most helpful to bring families in your community closer to him in the coming months.
2. Glance through the four sessions so that you have an overview of the months ahead, noting down resources that will take time to source.
3. Use the downloadable planning sheets to share this month's session with your core team in plenty of time to shape the ideas together to suit your own situation.
4. If you're meeting face to face with the team, talk about this month's theme, using the Messy team theme provided.
5. Tell God your worries.
6. Ensure that the whole extended team has copies of your final version of activities, together with the Bible reflection provided to give them the background they need. You could give them the link to the passage on **biblegateway.com** if you're not certain they have their own Bibles.
7. Include take-home ideas on handouts, texts or a Facebook page.
8. Print copies of the mealtime question
9.
10.

CW01045507

Planning suggestions

Contents

SESSION MATERIAL

Go to **messychurch.org.uk/getmessyjan19** to download all templates at A4 size, including a session planning sheet

In our next issue

May: Pray, pray, pray!

June: Dazzling disciples

July: Everything worships God

August: Created for community

Messy Minibooks

Are you looking for ways to help your Messy families engage with questions of faith together at home? We've produced our *Messy Minibooks* to help you do just that. These little illustrated books are colourful, quirky and jargon-free, meaning families can easily get together and work through the activities at their own pace.

Family Question Time is for those families just starting out on their journey, asking early questions and starting to explore.

Family Jesus Time is for those ready to take another step on the faith adventure. This book would make an ideal baptism gift.

Family Prayer Time is for those wanting to explore prayer. It offers simple prayers and addresses key questions such as 'Why should I pray?', 'Where should I pray?', 'How do I pray?' and 'What do I pray?'

Also available: *Christmas Family Time* and *Easter Family Time*.

Great price, with discounts for bulk orders. Go to brfonline.org.uk to order.

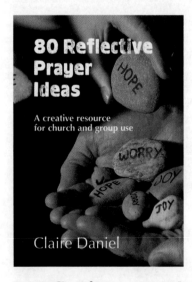

80 Reflective Prayer Ideas

ISBN 978 0 85746 673 0

£12.99

What ARE They Doing Down There?

ISBN 978 0 85746 693 8

£7.99

 @MessyChurchBRF

The Bible Reading Fellowship is a Registered Charity (233280)

One more musing on Messy Church being, well, church, and then I'll be quiet about it. It's very hard to be objective about this subject, mind you, having just looked through the photos from a Messy Church confirmation at Église Saint-Georges Messy Church in Quebec, kindly sent by Revd Neil Mancor. What do I see? Smiles, concentration, engagement; older and younger people; men and women; children, teens and adults; people of different skin colours – all together. I see food and drink – LOTS of food and drink! I see formality (mitres, a wimple, best dresses, ties and dog collars, kneeling and sitting in rows) alongside informality (T-shirts and jeans, lounging and chatting, gatherings round tables). I see colour, creativity, celebratory balloons and clear messages about Jesus that build up faith. I see pride, tenderness, prayer, excitement and confidence. I see a full building. Is it a community I want to be part of? It certainly is! Does it remind me of the early church just after Pentecost? It certainly does! Am I ridiculously and undeservedly proud to be a tiny, distant and insignificant part of that church family? I certainly am! Does it make all the papers theorising about ecclesiology seem totally irrelevant? Well, no: we need people to consider things rationally and impersonally and to help us be even more effective.

But when I spoke yesterday to a minister whose Messy Church was the first point of contact for a heroin addict, who went on to make a miraculous recovery through Jesus and the local church there; when I chatted to a Regional Coordinator, Sandra from Brussels, who told me about a lady who had found sanctuary in her local Messy Church with her child and has now asked to be baptised – then I want to thank God purely and simply for the unstoppable love he is pouring out on his planet and for the microscopic but happy part Messy Church is playing in that, whether or not it ticks every box of what makes something 'church'.

In the last issue of the magazine, we borrowed from Claire Dalpra's chapter in *Messy Church*

Theology (BRF, 2013), specifically about how 'church' is 'one, holy, catholic and apostolic'. We thought about being 'catholic' with a small 'c' and belonging to the wider church. The three other touchstones for 'church' are also helpful as we keep reflecting on how to be church more fully.

'One' – we can always do more to be as unified and healthy as we possibly can. One aspect of disunity that Messy Churches might be prone to is to mutter about members of our teams or families behind their backs. This is a habit which puts up a wall between 'us' and 'them' and is extraordinarily destructive. We need to work together on a culture which recognises that we are all part of the same body and, when one part suffers, we all suffer. If one part is maligned, we are all maligned. The early church was pretty rubbish at this, but knew they had to work on it!

'Holy' – this is the aspect of church that is about our relationship with God. It's always worth pausing, as a member of my own team said recently, to stop rushing around busily and thinking it all depends on us. In making space for God, we acknowledge that this is actually God's work; we get the chance to play a small part in it, but it's up to him what happens. It's a huge benefit! Holiness is such a relief from the heavy false god of our own importance. Let's get every team member to be a little oasis of holiness.

And 'apostolic' means that we have always got one eye, one hand, one foot, one wallet, one ear turned towards those who aren't already there. We face outwards, away from the actual Messy Church, to think always about how we can let other people know they are welcome there and to help each household be church at home, not just in the church building once a month. We don't atrophy into a face that always looks solely at what happens within the walls, but keep loose and limber neck muscles, forever turning outwards to what lies beyond.

Let's be the best church we can be.

Lucy Moore writes...

One, holy, catholic and apostolic church

Messy Baking at St Andrew's Church, Netherton
Ruth Filsak

Messy Baking is a new venture for St Andrew's Church, Netherton, Peterborough, and has been attended regularly by children from two years to four years with their parents. We have had between four and six families come along – small is good in this instance. It seems to be enjoyed by families attending and the leaders! We choose foods that the children can be very involved in making, include a cooking skill such as creaming butter and sugar or rubbing fat into flour, and ensure some healthy fruit or vegetables are part of the product. So far, we have made bread dough crocodiles and cheese scones (that was a mess, and too many things to do in one session), iced fairy cakes that had grated apple in and a fruit flan with a pastry base. The children showed great concentration and engagement in creating the food, and their smiles showed how much they enjoyed tasting it too. Adult helpers find they also learn some cooking skills!

This is being run in partnership with a Spurgeon's children's charity project, so is advertised through the local children's centres. We make it clear that it is a church activity, signpost families to our monthly Messy Church and aim to introduce a short God song/rhyme, but with no obligation to join in. In particular, we want families to feel welcomed into the church and comfortable being there.

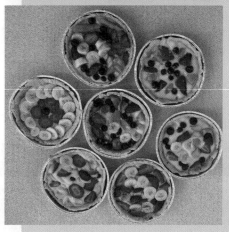

Messy Church @ Hinckley
Kate Roberts

After eight years of Messy Church @ Hinckley, Leicestershire, we had a change of leadership, and so we also wanted to find something new to do, especially to engage the older end of Messy Church (8+ years). We do a Messy Science table instead of cooking on alternate months. We start our planning with a Bible story and theme, and we come up with four craft tables, a prayer table and a science/cookery table that fits the theme.

Last month's theme was 'Would you believe it?' based on the story of Peter and Rhoda (Acts 12:12–15). The refraction Messy Science was a perfect fit – the kids were amazed (the disciples in the story were too) at seeing the arrows change direction once looked at through the glass of 'magic liquid'. The kids then drew their own pictures, e.g. a winking smiley face, and predicted what they would see before and after. We then talked about why things sometimes seem like 'magic' but that the 'magic' can sometimes be explained (by science) or sometimes not (by faith in God). The older kids were then shown what is actually happening, in science terms, to explain why we see things differently.

They took home their drawn pictures to try again and to show family.

We keep the Messy Science theme going by always having white lab coats for the kids to wear and they get to put on science goggles for those experiments that involve explosions! Next time, they're going to take a celery experiment home to see how water is absorbed over time (capillary action). We're hopefully keeping things a bit 'out there' – we want to keep them guessing and wondering what they're doing next at Messy Church.

Banyule Network of Uniting Churches

Revd Sandy Brodine

We are fortunate in the Banyule Network of Uniting Churches to have not one, not two, but three professors of Science, as well as quite a few other science professionals who were keen to join our regular team in planning Messy Science for both of our Messy Churches: at Heidelberg and at Ivanhoe, in suburban Melbourne, Australia, earlier this year.

We had a fascinating planning meeting focusing on what inspired these three professors of deep faith to embark on a life passionately working in science and thinking about how we could share that passion for the scientific endeavour and love of God with our Messy communities.

The crux was this: science is about wonder and asking questions. It's about testing and trying out ideas. Sometimes those prove to be right and sometimes they are wrong. But whether right or wrong, they teach the scientist something more about the world that God created. And each new thing they learn deepens their wonder and awe for the creator who made the world.

Professor Ian Gordon, a medical statistician, led the kids in an exploration of how gravity worked. They tested out different things, to see which fell the fastest. The kids found this quite fascinating and several were still asking their parents questions for a week.

Professor Mike Clarke, a zoologist, brought along a wonderful collection of gum leaves and shells. He showed us the 'lerp' that grows on the leaves and explained how insects make it. We wondered about what we could see through the magnifying glasses. We looked at the tiny seeds that come from a river red gum tree and were astonished that everything needed to make an enormous tree is created in a tiny speck of a seed.

We also had fun learning about surface tension with a challenge to make a bubble wand to blow a square bubble, and about polymers while we made fluffy slime. It was a wonderful, Messy exploration of all things scientific: wondering about how God's world works, and the God who created it.

During the celebration time at Ivanhoe, Ian and Mike spoke about what inspires them about the world and about God. The kids asked some fascinating questions, including where the wind comes from, what they thought about creation and evolution and how the sun made the wind blow. It was wonderful hearing kids from preschool up to late primary ages engage thoughtfully and intelligently with the material that was shared with them. The grown-ups were all challenged too!

We were really grateful for the enthusiastic way that our scientists shared their love of God and science with us all. It really helped us to think about God and faith in a very different way. Professor Ian Gordon has told me that he'd like to do a mathematic-themed Messy Church in 2019… I'm a tiny bit terrified, but willing to give it a go!

Messy weddings... and so much more

Lucy Moore

We loved seeing the Messy weddings that took place last year to celebrate the royal wedding and the wedding at Cana. Has there ever been so much confetti cannoned about? Were wedding hats ever so extravagant? Bouquets so… abundant? Dresses so… mesmerising?

Perhaps even more exciting was the real, actual, genuine Messy wedding that took place, appropriately enough, at the church where Messy Church first began, St Wilf's in Cowplain, near Portsmouth, in Hampshire. Robin Jones and Jenny Dickin, both leaders of the Messy Church there and involved in many other aspects of the church family life, met, fell in love, got engaged and decided that a Messy Church wedding was the right way for them. I was privileged to be invited and saw for myself what an actual Messy wedding could look like.

Of course, there were the normal traumas: what does one wear? A wedding is a special occasion, but a Messy wedding might well be less neat and tidy than most weddings, where the worst thing that could happen to my limited stock of posh frocks would be a spilt glass of fizzy wine. At a Messy wedding, frankly, even I dared not imagine the worst. I compromised and took a Messy apron to wear over my finery.

We arrived in good time. Robin welcomed us in his usual T-shirt and gave the team a quick talk to set the scene, then went back to sorting out the sound system; you need to appreciate that both Robin and Jenny are hands-on people who hate pomp, ceremony or pretentiousness and their wedding reflected that. Family and friends of all ages, from about ten years upwards, were hard at work slicing up raw Danish pastries for cooking and keeping the flow of hospitality going. I found the activity I was running. The passage Jenny and Robin had chosen was from Proverbs and was a great romp of lessons to be learned for marriage from the animal kingdom: ants, rock badgers and the like.

As guests arrived, they were greeted with tray after tray of pastries, coffee and tea, and left to have fun over the eight or so different activities. Jenny arrived, looking, of course, gorgeous, at the advertised start of the wedding, 11.30, so she too could enjoy the refreshments and the activities. By 11.55, we were all sitting in rows like a normal wedding. Helium balloons decorated the church and gave it a party feel. I wondered where Jenny and Robin were, glanced over my shoulder and saw Robin changing into a long-sleeved shirt (a huge concession) and Jenny setting the table for lunch. They walked up the aisle together and the ceremony continued in a relaxed, happy, participatory vein: for the intercessions, prayers were written on luggage tags and tied to the balloon strings, which gave every balloon a lop-sided

All photos on this page by Jenny Dickin

weightiness that added to the fun. Friends played the music. After the ceremony, a hog roast filled up the corners not already filled by the stacks of snacks beforehand (with options for every dietary need under the sun – all part of hospitality). There were minimal speeches, but the church did manage to present the couple with a stunning handmade patchwork quilt featuring significant fabrics. The wedding was joyful. It was down to earth. It was uplifting. It was family. It was a feast. It was a celebration for people of all ages, bursting with hospitality and creativity, and shouting of Jesus. It was very Messy Church.

While we're on the subject of life events, let's talk christenings and funerals, too. We know some denominations don't baptise at all, but many do. For christenings in a Messy Church setting, you might want to check out the suggestions and ideas on our website by doing a search on 'baptism', as the scene is changing and developing all the time. It's encouraging that things have moved on so much over the last 15 years. There are still mountains to climb but, by and large, there is now much greater acceptance of the fact that Messy Church can be an appropriate setting in which to baptise members of that Messy Church. I remember years ago that a vicar insisted a Messy family had to attend Sunday church for six months before he would baptise their child, even though they were faithful members of the weekday Messy Church in his church. The Liturgical Commission of the Church of England (possibly still slightly traumatised from having worked on a Messy Communion) took it for granted that the sample baptism services, described in a publication on baptism, needed to include a Messy Church baptism.

And joyful occasions aren't the only ones that need marking or celebrating. When members of your Messy Church face the reality of somebody near to them dying, please don't avoid the subject of death or pretend it isn't painful. Meet that family in their grief and help everybody understand what death in a Christian context can mean and how to look after each other throughout their bereavement. It's best to build this into your existing plans, so death becomes a natural part of life and families already know that church is the place to come with pain as well as with joy. You'll find that back copies of *Get Messy!* (available as PDFs from **brfonline. org.uk**) have sessions on remembrance and on our heavenly home. And coming out soon will be a wonderful resource book from Joanna Collicutt and the Messy Church team about death and dying and how we can talk helpfully about this difficult subject with families and children with pastoral and theological integrity. There will be five Messy sessions in it, exploring different aspects of death or bereavement in the usual hands-on way.

Messy confirmations are happening too, as mentioned on page 5. Johnathon Pyne, from Basingstoke, was confirmed by the Bishop of Basingstoke. Johnathon (15) said, 'I want a Messy confirmation because I feel it is more interesting than a bog-standard confirmation. I also feel that the Messy congregation is more my faith family than the Sunday congregation. I didn't want to have a normal one; I wanted something different and special to me because I am special. I also feel that it's easier to invite my non-Christian friends to Messy Church rather than traditional church.'

What might this all mean for the future? How will ministers and church leaders be trained to appreciate, celebrate and develop these tentative starting places wisely? What resources does BRF need to create, with the Messy network's help, to provide a rich bank of material to draw on? What would help you in your unique setting, to make sure Messy Church provides a fruitful framework for marking life's events? How can each one be another step closer to a relationship with Jesus?

Sue Noonan

Sue Noonan

Jane Leadbetter

Photos of other Messy wedding celebrations

Discipleship Pilot

© Thinkstock

How is your Discipleship Pilot going? Remember this isn't about adding burdens to an already-laden team. It's about doing what we already do more intentionally and about keeping the bigger picture in view rather than being content with short-term easy-wins and a limited belief in what God wants to do with your Messy Church. You may indeed be trying out some exciting Messy Extra, like Johannah Myers' intergenerational Messy Home Groups, of which she has seven running in her church! But, equally, you may be faithfully sending home an idea for families to use at home to help them pray or read the Bible or talk about God. Or you might just be taking a moment before each Messy Church to ask God to open your eyes to the full life he longs for, for every person who comes, younger or older.

Make sure we know how things have gone, whether it's been a success or an apparent failure, or just a bit 'meh'. Together, we can build up a picture of what works so that other Messy Churches can take the paths you have pioneered. And remember, we've always known this is going to take a long time, is about relationships far more than programmes and will impact on our lives as well as on the lives of people nearer the start of their faith adventure.

If you haven't got round to it yet, do check out the Discipleship Pilot on the website (**messychurch.org.uk/messy-discipleship-pilot**) and use it as a tool to get your team thinking and praying about your next step.

Youth column

Two junior team members from Old Town, Swindon Messy Church

Daniel (12)

I love art and playing the guitar. I first started going to Messy Church with my parents, who are on the core team of our Messy Church. I now help to run the activities each month. My favourite part of Messy Church is helping others with the activities and the Messy tea. My favourite part of being on the team is the feeling of being useful while having fun at the same time.

If I were to describe Messy Church to someone in a sentence, I would say: Messy Church is a great way to interact with people and to learn about God through fun and interesting activities.

Photo by Old Town, Swindon, Messy Church

Robyn (12)

My name is Robyn and I am twelve years old. I am in Year 7 at school and my hobbies include playing the flute, going to Guides and looking after my two guinea pigs. I have a younger sister who is nine.

I first went to Messy Church when it started in Old Town, Swindon. I went to the first ever one and have been going ever since. I was seven when it started. I like all the crafts, particularly the junk modelling. We have made some great team models, including a Noah's Ark with cardboard roll sheep.

I am now a helper. I help in the drama section, where we act out a Bible story. So far, we have done the creation story and the nativity. I like helping as it is good to be a team. We all work together and have fun. I would like it if more people my age got involved.

I would describe Messy Church to others as Bible-themed crafting, service and eating.

#MCIC19
#discipleship

International Conference

It's nearly here! May 2019 will see about 200 Messy Church leaders gathering from around the world to celebrate what God is doing in this movement. Through the disorientation of being in the lap of luxury (instead of on their hands and knees chiselling dried peas off the bottom of pews), delegates from different nations will be making new friends, renewing old friendships and listening to speakers who will challenge them and send their thoughts down new pathways. They'll be taking part in a fun-packed programme designed to provide new ideas and new ways of thinking, to affirm half-formulated wonderings and to give space in all the activity simply to rest in God's hands and be revived for the next step of their adventure with him.

The whole programme is based around **#discipleship**, however you choose to understand that in a Messy Church setting. Through thinking and talking together across so many countries, denominations and traditions, we expect to make great strides towards approaches and attitudes that will help every Messy Church.

We are so looking forward to hearing the wisdom of our two speakers. Claire Dalpra is part of the Church Army Research Unit and has been researching discipleship in Messy Church over the last twelve months. She'll be presenting her findings and helping us explore the implications. Claire and her team are highly respected, professional yet sympathetic researchers and we can't wait to find out how her work can help us develop our Messy Churches.

Andrew Roberts is a Methodist minister who has been developing new ways for churches to use his book *Holy Habits* (Malcolm Down Publishing, 2016) to help their members grow closer to God through everyday habits of holiness. With a wealth of experience at grassroots level as well as at national level, Andrew has been a friend of Messy Church for many years and his thoughts will be a great help to us.

But we all know that a lot of the learning will come in the gaps and in the conversations over coffee and meals and relaxed moments, just as it does at Messy Church itself. Jane Leadbetter and Barry Brand (author of *Extreme Crafts for Messy Churches*) are planning bonfires and other wild outdoor activities. (Lucy is preparing lengthy risk assessments.) Alison Thurlow (leader of the renowned Yate St Nix Messy Church), Stephen Fischbacher (from Fischy Music) and our very own Martyn Payne will be weaving a supportive hammock of prayer, music and worship. Other members of the planning team will be making hospitality, creativity and fun happen all through the workshops, activities and downtime so that everyone enjoys the fullest possible experience. And we may even get a little… messy.

Survey follow-up

Thanks to everyone who took part in our Leaders' and Families' surveys last year. The results are in and are very encouraging. There's a lot to learn from this, so here is some data to ponder, along with some practical suggestions that you might like to do or have a think about with your team. Let us know what works (and what doesn't work) by emailing messychurch@brf.org.uk.

Although 85% of leaders feel Messy Church is drawing people closer to God, only **55%** feel **it is making disciples**. *(Q21 leaders' survey, slide 23)*

- As a team, have everyone write down and then share what you think it means to be a disciple of Jesus.

- Have a go at the Discipleship Pilot (**messychurch. org.uk/messy-discipleship-pilot**) together as a team to think about how you can intentionally be doing discipleship at your Messy Church.

- Tell your church leadership how you feel you've grown in your discipleship through your involvement with Messy Church and ask them to pray for you.

Two-thirds of Messy Church families feel that Messy Church is a **comfortable place** in which they can **discuss their beliefs and doubts**. *(Q11 families' survey, slide 35)*

- Have questions out on the tables during the meal to help people continue to talk about the Bible story.

- Have a couple of 'floaters' on the team who can wander around and chat to people.

- Write down your resolution to talk about your beliefs and doubts to one person at the next Messy Church.

Approximately **15%** of Messy Churches have done a **Holy Communion** and/or **baptism** at their Messy Church. *(Q18 leaders' survey, slide 24)*

- Suggest to your minister that a suitable month to celebrate a Messy Church Communion this year would be…

- Have a look at the Communion pack the Messy Church team has put together on our website (**messychurch.org.uk/holy-communion**).

- Ask at your next Messy Church if anyone young or old would like to talk about being christened.

64% of Messy Church families expect they will **continue to come to Messy Church for the next 5–10 years**. *(Q17 families' survey, slide 38)*

- Ask a ten-year-old what is the messiest thing they've always wanted to do, then see if you can make that activity fit the theme of your next Messy Church session.

- Put up a graffiti wall with a sad face and a happy face and invite people to write what they do and don't like about your Messy Church.

- Commit to praying for one family once a day for one month.

Only **40%** of leaders have done any Messy Church **training**.   *(Q25 leaders' survey, slide 26)*

- Check out the Training page on the Messy Church website (**messychurch.org.uk/events-and-training**). Contact your denominational training officer and ask if there's any funding to host a training session.

- Keep an eye out on the Events page on our website (**messychurch.org.uk/events/all**) for any training sessions nearby, or ring us up and ask for one.

- Ask your Regional Coordinator for a Messy Meet-up for local leaders and offer to provide the cake!

Amazingly, over **85%** of Messy Church leaders feel that **God is using Messy Church to draw people closer to him**.
(Q14 leaders' survey, slide 21)

- As a team, talk about how God is drawing *you* closer to him through Messy Church.

- Include a response time in your celebration: 'Talk to the person you came with about what you like best in this story.'

- Resolve to make one of your activities each time a prayer activity.

Over **two-thirds** of Messy Church families **talk about God at home together**, and some also **read the Bible** and **pray together**.
(Q14 families' survey, slide 37)

- Give everyone one of the Messy minibooks. (They're created for families to work through together.)

- Put together a display of Bibles suitable for families at different stages. Your local Christian bookshop may be able to help with this.

- Have an activity table that is a space to share ideas of how to pray as a family at bedtime.

Over **85%** of Messy Church leaders feel **confident sharing the gospel** with those who come to their Messy Church.
(Q17 leaders' survey, slide 19)

- As a team, share the best conversation you've had about Jesus at Messy Church.

- Discuss the activity questions together as a team before your Messy Church and share what your thoughts are.

- Have an occasional 'Everyday God' slot, where someone talks in the celebration about how their faith makes a difference in the way they live their normal life.

Half of the families who come to Messy Church would like to **know more about Jesus!**
(Q18 families' survey, slide 39)

- Stick a sticky jewel on to a crown outline for every person you can name who comes to your Messy Church and thank God for them.

- Ask your families what aspect of God or being a Christian they would like to know more about.

- Set up an intergenerational home group where you can explore the Bible together and build community once a month for six months.

A third of Messy Church families would like to be a **part of the team** in some capacity.
(Q21 families' survey, slide 41)

- When you next need help with something at Messy Church, deliberately ask someone unexpected, unlikely or new.

- Ask your older children and teens how they would like to help lead.

- What might make it hard for a new person to join your team? Is there anything you can do about that specific thing?

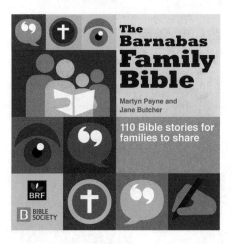

Bible overview

And now for Part 2 of our Bible overview… In the September issue, we offered a range of activities to share with your Messy congregations. Now, here's a brave attempt to cram the broad sweep of the Bible narrative into a couple of pages or so, taken from *The Barnabas Family Bible* by Martyn Payne and Jane Butcher. How about giving this out as a take-home idea (go to **messychurch.org.uk/getmessyjan19** to download copies) or using part of it during the celebration time?

In the beginning, God made the heavens and the earth. He began by saying, 'Let there be light,' and there was light. Next, he made the water and that was good. Then God made the land and he saw that that was good. Afterwards came the sun, moon and stars to give light for the day and the night. This too was good. Then he filled the waters with fish of all kinds and the air with birds and he said that that was good. Finally, he made the creatures and he also made people – you and me – and put them in charge of his world, to look after it. When God saw everything that he had made, he said that it was very good. When he had finished creating the world, God rested.

God made everything good but soon the world began to go bad. People chose not to care for God's world or even for each other. God was sad and decided to start all over again by sending a flood.

Only Noah's family truly believed in God, so they were kept safe in a boat called an ark. On board were representatives of all the animals that God had made, so that God could fill his cleaned-up world with life again after the flood.

When the flood was over, Noah and his family and the animals came out. They remembered to thank God for all that he had done. Then God gave them a sign that he would never stop loving his world and its people in future. He gave them a rainbow. God kept his promise. He never stopped loving people. He wanted to help them trust him, whatever happened. Once, he spoke to a man called Abraham and told him and his wife Sarah to set out on a dangerous journey across the desert to a new place to live, called Canaan. Abraham could not see God, but he believed that God was always close. God looked after them on their long journey. He gave them a safe place to live. He also promised them that he would give them a son and that from this son would come a family and a great nation. In that nation, one day, a very special person would be born, who would bring God's love to the whole world. God's family would be world-big and contain as many people as there are stars in the sky or grains of sand in the desert. God kept his promise.

God's people didn't find it easy to trust God. They often made mistakes and often deliberately chose to go their own way, ending up in trouble. Many years after Abraham, they found themselves as slaves in Egypt. Their situation seemed hopeless, but God did not forget them. He sent Moses to bring them to freedom. The Pharaoh in Egypt let them go only when a terrible thing happened. All the eldest boy children of the Egyptians, including the Pharaoh's own child, died. God's people, however, were kept safe. They had put lambs' blood around the doors of their houses, so the angel of death had passed over them and they were saved. Moses led them across the Red Sea to freedom.

God's people had been in such a rush to leave, however, that there had been no time to bake proper bread for the journey. Their bread had no yeast or leaven in it, so it was flat. They called it unleavened bread. Whenever they ate this bread, they remembered how God had brought them from slavery to freedom.

God guided Moses and he led them through the desert to a new home. God gave them miraculous food to eat and water to drink; but even then, some of them began to doubt God's love. It was so easy to forget the best way to live. So God called Moses up a mountain and gave him the law, which included the ten commandments. These ten rules would help people to know how to come close to God. They told the people how to love God and to love other people. After a journey of 40 years, the people were finally ready to come to God's promised land. This was the place where they would be safe. In order to get into this land, they had one more thing to do. They needed to cross the River Jordan. It seemed impossible but Joshua, who had taken over from Moses as leader, trusted God to show them how. The priests went out into the water first, carrying the great golden chest that contained the ten commandments, and they stood in the middle of the river. As soon as the priests were there, the River Jordan began to dry up so that the people could cross safely. After many years of walking through the desert, they could walk into God's special home for them. Their feet were dusty from their desert journey but as they crossed the wet riverbed they were cleaned, ready for a new beginning.

God kept on looking after his people in the new land, but there were so many temptations for the people to forget him and go their own way. There were great leaders and kings, such as David and Solomon, but even they didn't always choose God's way. They built special places to worship God – even a golden temple in Jerusalem – but they began to forget that God was everywhere, not just in a building.

God sent special people to remind them of his love and warn them of the dangers of turning away from his love. These were called prophets, but not everyone listened to their messages. Finally, God decided that the only way to show his love to them was to come and live with them himself. God decided to wrap himself up very small, and he quietly entered his own world as a tiny baby.

God had planned this all along as the way that he was going to show people what he was really like and how he could keep them safe for ever. God was inside a human body, and we call him Jesus.

Jesus shone bright with God's light. When he was about 30 years old, he went to the River Jordan, where his cousin John was baptising people. He asked John to baptise him. John was surprised. He knew how special Jesus was. Jesus should baptise him! However, Jesus insisted and so he went down into the water and came out again. People nearby said they heard God's voice; others saw a dove coming close to Jesus. Jesus was showing everyone the way to start a new life with God. The washing of baptism became a picture of how people enter into the safe place of trusting God forever.

Jesus began teaching people about God and his ways. Crowds gathered to listen. Once, he was speaking to a great crowd of men, women and children on a mountainside in Galilee. He told them about what things are like when God is king. He described the sort of lives God's people should lead. He said that people would be happy if they knew that they needed God; happy if they were sad about being far from him; happy if they always put others first. They would be happy if they longed for what was good and right, and happy if they were kind and said 'no' to all that was bad; happy if they were people who made peace. Everyone else might think they were crazy and laugh at them, but this was the only way to be happy and make God happy too.

Jesus said and did amazing things. Everyone knew that he was special and that he was showing them what God was like. However, very few really knew who he was. He called himself by many names. Once he said he was the light; on other occasions he called himself the good shepherd and the way; and once he described himself as the door. But Jesus knew that the only way for him to rescue people from the badness that keeps spoiling our lives was to go to Jerusalem and to die on a cross. Everyone now who comes to God through this door can be safe and rescued from all that is bad. The cross gave people the power to choose to do what is right.

After three days, Jesus was seen alive again in a new Easter way. He could now always be there for his people, to lead them into what was good and true. Although people could not see him, he was there in a new invisible way and people followed him. He wanted everyone to be filled with light as he was filled with light, and to take God's love out into the world so that more and more people would become part of God's new beginning. God's promise to Abraham was coming true. God's family was growing and growing and was becoming as many as the stars in the sky or the grains of sand in the desert.

Jesus wanted everyone to remember him so that they would not forget how to come close to God wherever they were. He had given them a way to do this – not a rainbow this time, but a simple meal to share together. It had first been part of the meal he had eaten with his friends the night before he died. There had been bread to eat and wine to drink. Every time Christians eat and drink in this way, they remember Jesus. They remember how he died and then came back to life to be with everyone everywhere forever.

The story ends with a new beginning. The first creation will be over and, because of Jesus, all that is bad and that spoils God's world will be washed away. Everyone will be able to choose to be safe in Jesus. The Bible promises that God will make a new heaven and a new earth, full of light. This is the light of God and of Jesus his Son. All that was broken will be mended and all that was painful will be healed. This is how the Bible ends, but really it is just the first page of a new book that will go on forever.

Messy Church values quiz

1 What are the five Messy Church values?

   a. Fun, mess, glitter, glue, sausages, pasta, innumeracy.

   b. Eschatology, evangelism, erudition, epiclesis, episiotomy.

   c. Christ-centred, creativity, all-age, hospitality, celebration.

2 What's the point of having values rather than a strict definition of Messy Church?

   a. It scores well on the ecclesial pretentiousness scale.

   b. It's in keeping with the generally wet, woolly, ultra-liberal, ill-defined, anything-goes nature of Messy Church.

   c. It keeps the integrity of the Messy Church concept while encouraging local contextualisation.

3 Have you discovered the useful Bristol Self-Assessment Toolkit on the Discipleship page of messychurch.org.uk, based on the five values?

   a. There's a Messy Church website?

   b. There's a Discipleship page?

   c. We're using it with our team to get loads of good ideas for developing our Messy Church.

   d. You're sure there's a Discipleship page?

4 Being Christ-centred involves:

   a. Geometric tools to discover exactly where the centre of our church is and putting a cross there.

   b. Ignoring any families who arrive because we're busy praying.

   c. Reorientating our hearts, expectations and hopes towards Jesus in every part of Messy Church.

5 Creativity involves:

   a. Something pink to take home and stick on the fridge.

   b. Burying the church building under several strata of paint, glitter and half-chewed decorated biscuits.

   c. Giving space to the creative Spirit of God alive in every human being, including the team.

6 Being all-age involves:

   a. Dumbing down.

   b. Kidnapping residents of the local care home and incarcerating them in Messy Church.

   c. Enjoying how beautiful church is when we are with people who are different from us.

7 Hospitality involves:

   a. Leering obsequiously as people arrive.

   b. Getting people fed as cheaply as possible.

   c. Embodying the welcome of God to his beloved people.

8 Celebration involves:

   a. Manic, high-energy entertainment at every opportunity.

   b. Just the nice, happy gospel stories – not anything involving sin, blood, judgement, animals getting hurt or Jesus saying something puzzling.

   c. Putting the joy back into church.

Mostly 'c's
Well, of course. You're a *Get Messy!* subscriber. What do you expect?

Mostly other answers
You're kidding, right?

Transforming lives with spare change
Help Messy Churches thrive with our new collection boxes

Most of us have a bit of loose change lying around. Wouldn't it be great if you could put it to good use and help transform lives and communities through the Christian faith?

Here at The Bible Reading Fellowship (BRF), the home of Messy Church, we've introduced collection boxes to make it super easy for you to support Messy Churches around the UK and overseas, particularly those that are small, new or based in deprived areas. The boxes are small, lightweight and easy to construct and can be used at home, in your church or elsewhere.

To get you in the collecting mood, we thought we'd put together a list of ideas to help you get the most out of your collection for Messy Church. After all, we wouldn't want you to make a mess of it. **brf.org.uk/collectionboxes**

Eight ideas to help you run collections for Messy Church

1. Read all about it!
Spreading the word is the key to success, so make sure you let people know about your collection. Where possible, put a notice in any church newsletters or parish magazines.

2. You can't miss it
Put your box in a prominent place where people are sure to see it. At Messy Church, this is likely to be your welcome or refreshments table. At home, it might be by the front door, so you remember to slip a few coins inside when you get home.

3. Fundraise for us
Run a fundraising activity for Messy Church and use your box to collect donations. Coffee mornings are always popular, or you could try running Messy Splat featured in the January to April 2018 issue of *Get Messy!* Contact us at **giving@brf.org.uk** or call **+44 (0)1865 319700** to find out more.

4. Ahoy, me hearties, it's time for a treasure hunt!
Coins can get everywhere – under sofa cushions, in pockets, at the back of drawers . Hunt for this buried treasure around your home or church and deposit what you find in your box.

5. Collect the pennies
We receive small change from many of the purchases we make. Consider putting it in your collection box rather than your purse or wallet. This works particularly well for collections in the home.

6. Skip the niceties
Could you go without that daily cappuccino, chocolate bar or newspaper? Whatever your 'nice to have' is, think about going without and popping the money in your collection box instead. You might choose to do this as a Messy Church around Christmastime or for Lent.

7. Make a commitment
Get everyone in your Messy Church to pledge £1 next time they come along or, if you're running a collection at home, commit to paying in a small amount each week. You'll be surprised how quickly it all adds up!

8. The naughty box
We all have bad habits, be it burping, biting your nails or something else. Collecting 'fines' is a classic way to fill up your box and Messy Church families can have great fun spotting each other's bad habits and calling them to account!

To find out more about our collection boxes, visit brf.org.uk/collectionboxes
or get in touch by calling +44 (0)1865 319700

Session material: January

 Go to **messychurch.org.uk/ getmessyjan19** to download all templates at A4 size, including a session planning sheet

#discipleship: individual

Messy reflection by Jean Pienaar

Every year Jesus' parents travelled to Jerusalem for the Feast of Passover. When he was twelve years old, they went up as they always did for the Feast. When it was over and they left for home, the child Jesus stayed behind in Jerusalem, but his parents didn't know it. Thinking he was somewhere in the company of pilgrims, they journeyed for a whole day and then began looking for him among relatives and neighbours. When they didn't find him, they went back to Jerusalem looking for him.

The next day they found him in the Temple seated among the teachers, listening to them and asking questions. The teachers were all quite taken with him, impressed with the sharpness of his answers. But his parents were not impressed; they were upset and hurt.

His mother said, 'Young man, why have you done this to us? Your father and I have been half out of our minds looking for you.'

He said, 'Why were you looking for me? Didn't you know that I had to be here, dealing with the things of my Father?' But they had no idea what he was talking about.

So he went back to Nazareth with them, and lived obediently with them. His mother held these things dearly, deep within herself. And Jesus matured, growing up in both body and spirit, blessed by both God and people.
Luke 2:41–52 (MSG)

This occasion was not the first time Jesus had made the trip to Jerusalem to celebrate the Passover. His family would have been familiar with the crowds of people, traffic jams and crowd control as a few million people came to Jerusalem for the feast each year. (Exact numbers are unknown, but historians estimate between three million and four million Jews from the diaspora descended on Jerusalem for holy days.) But now, Jesus is a twelve-year-old boy and has reached the awkward stage of preadolescence. Science tells us that the brain changes during puberty, which may explain the heightened emotions, impulsive decisions and risk-taking behaviour at this time.

In many ways, it is not entirely surprising that Jesus stayed back in Jerusalem while his parents assumed that he was with them. Having three sons, with two at the start of their teenage years, I can understand Jesus' behaviour and his oblivion to any concern his parents might have had regarding his whereabouts.

Some societies intentionally celebrate the transition from childhood to adulthood. In the process, a group of mentors or elders (in addition to the parents) commit themselves to standing alongside the child, acknowledging the beginning of their journey to adulthood, and providing him/her with a set of role models. The African proverb that 'it takes a village to raise a child' bears this out.

As parents and grandparents (and aunts and uncles and godparents…), we need to ensure that our young people are safe from those who might want to harm them or lead them astray. Quite deliberately, we can gather and encourage a group of Christian mentors for our children and pre-teens, who can help them negotiate the transition towards adulthood. Messy Church can provide the safe environment for neighbours and people of the area to form part of the village needed to raise the child.

#discipleship: team

Messy health check

Which people groups in your community are you not reaching through Messy Church? Is there anything you can do to invite them?

Messy team theme

- Where do you go to learn more about Father God?
- How do you welcome and include others in the family of God?
- How do we extend that to people who are not yet a part of our Messy community here?

How does this session help people grow in Christ?

In this passage, we see the briefest glimpse of Jesus' childhood: a snapshot of his life between birth and the beginning of his ministry, and yet here is also a profound statement about who he was and where he found his identity. In this incident, Jesus revealed his true identity as both a son of an earthly family and member of the community gathered to celebrate Passover in Jerusalem, and the Son of God who found his place with his Father in the temple.

@MessyChurchBRF

Where I belong by Becky May

Through this session, we look directly at Jesus' example and explore how we, through him, belong not only to a physical family, but also to one another in our Messy Church family and worldwide family of God, as children of Father God.

#discipleship: families

Mealtime card

- What do you remember, enjoy or look forward to about being twelve?
- Where do you most love to be and why?
- How do you know when you 'belong'?

Take-home idea

Visit a church building and spend some time there as a family. Talk about the different ways it helps you to connect with God, or whether there is a different place you like to go to feel close to God.

Father God, thank you that we can find special places to go where we can feel close to you. Amen

Question to start and end the session

So… what does it mean to find a place where you belong?

#discipleship: extra

Hold a marshmallow-toasting and storytelling evening campfire.

1

2

Activities

1. Model temple

You will need: cardboard boxes of different sizes; sticky tape; scissors; pictures of the temple in Jerusalem at the time of Jesus (various images can be found online)

Work together to create a large cardboard model of the temple, as Jesus would have known it. Look carefully at all the images to try to include the different elements in the model.

Talk about why the temple was so important to Jews at this time and the significance of the different parts of the building.

2. Jesus as a twelve-year-old

You will need: paper; scissors; glue sticks; Christmas cards with nativity scenes; pencils; crayons; felt-tip pens

Fold a sheet of paper in half and label one half 'Jesus as a baby' and the other 'Jesus as a twelve-year-old'. Choose a picture of Jesus as a baby from the Christmas cards to cut out and stick it on the first half of your paper. Imagine what Jesus would have been like as a twelve-year-old and draw this on the other side of the paper.

Talk about what we imagine Jesus would have been like as a twelve-year-old boy. In what ways would he have been like us? In what ways would he have been different?

3. Graffiti wall questions

You will need: large sheets of paper, stuck up on the wall; marker pens

Write 'Big God Questions' in the middle of the paper before the session begins. On the paper, graffiti (anonymously) your big questions about God or for God.

Talk about how Jesus was in the temple talking to the leaders and asking them questions. Talk about some of the questions that are added to the wall and perhaps return to them in the celebration or at another time.

Session material: January

4. Seder plate tasting

You will need: food to go on a Seder plate: *karpas* **(parsley),** *maror* **(bitter herb such as horseradish root or just the stem of a romaine lettuce),** *charoset* **(mixture of apples, pears and walnuts – use apple sauce if you can't source this),** *zeroah* **(piece of roasted lamb),** *matzah* **(flat savoury biscuit),** *beitzah* **(hard-boiled egg); Seder plates or normal plates**

A Seder plate, used during the festival of Passover, consists of different foods that remind the Jewish people of their time as slaves in Egypt and God's miraculous rescue. For example, the bitter herbs remind them of their suffering in Egypt; the *charoset* looks like bricks and mortar, which they would have made as slaves; the lamb represents the Passover offering. Set out the Seder plate, either on a special plate designed for this purpose, or on a plain plate, and taste some of the different elements.

Talk about how Jesus had travelled with his family to enjoy the Passover celebration and how this was the meal they would share together. Talk about what each of the elements represents, to us and to them. (Further explanation can be found at **godventure.co.uk/news/2976**.)

5. Scrolls

You will need: wooden lolly sticks; paper; pens; glue sticks; ribbon

On the paper, write or print the words from Luke 2:52 (NLT): 'Jesus grew in wisdom and in stature and in favour with God and all the people.' Glue a lolly stick along the top and bottom of the paper. When dried, roll the paper in from both ends to meet in the middle. Tie the scroll securely with a ribbon.

Talk about how the leaders in the temple would have been studying the Torah (the Old Testament), written on scrolls.

6. Family coat of arms

You will need: wooden or card shield shapes; pencils; paint; collage materials; glue; scissors

Work together as a family group to create a shield with images and symbols that represent things that are important to your family – things you all relate to, such as shared hobbies, the meaning of your names, etc. – using an assortment of collage materials.

Talk about how it feels to belong within your family and how you identify together. Jesus was a member of his earthly family and the Jewish community, sharing their festival together, and also belonged to his heavenly Father God.

7. Height chart

You will need: wallpaper border rolls; scissors; wooden pegs; metre rules; marker pens

Cut a length of border paper. Using the metre rule and marker pen, make markings along one edge of the paper, perhaps at 5 cm or 10 cm intervals. Take one peg for each member of your family and write their names on them. At home, you can set up your height chart and measure each member of your family.

Talk about how we change as we grow up. Did Jesus think he was more grown-up than Mary and Joseph were ready for?

8. Map prayers

You will need: a map of the local area; stickers

Find somewhere on the map that is special or important to you and stick a sticker on, as you pray for that place. It could be your own home, the home of someone special to you, your school, the place that Messy Church meets or somewhere else.

Talk about why you have chosen to pray for this place and what, specifically, you want to pray. Why does this place matter to you?

9. People web

You will need: paper plates; scissors; hole punches; wool

Cut the centre away from the paper plates and punch holes all around the edge. Tie a length of wool through one hole and begin threading the wool back and forth across the plate to create a web pattern. You could repeat with a different-coloured wool in order to continue the web.

Talk about the way that each of us is connected to one another in this Messy Church community.

10. Learning from the best

You will need: an appropriate selection of tools and materials, as detailed below, perhaps brought along by your Messy Church families

Invite members of your Messy Church to bring along a particular skill or hobby that they have, to demonstrate and teach to other people. This will work best if you specifically ask a few members of your group beforehand to bring something you know they are interested in. Try to include activity leaders of different ages or generations. Activities could include a craft such as knitting or pyrography, a skill such as fixing a bike or playing a musical instrument, etc.

Where I belong by Becky May

Talk about the different things we learn from one another. What has someone older than you taught you? What about someone who is younger than you? Jesus and the temple leaders learned from one another.

5

6

7

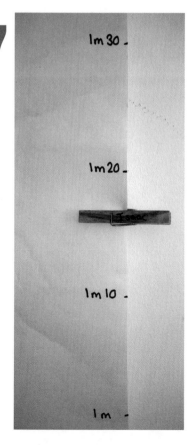

Celebration

You will need: three volunteers: a baby, a twelve-year-old and a 30-year-old adult

Gather together in your celebration area and begin by presenting a baby to the group, saying:

We have recently celebrated Christmas, when we remembered Jesus as a tiny baby, just like _____ here. We also know lots about what Jesus did when he was an adult like _____. (*Invite your adult volunteer to the front.*)

But you see, there's quite a gap between being a baby and being a grown-up! (*Point to each of your volunteers in turn.*) Actually, lots of you are in this in-between part at the moment, aren't you? I wonder what Jesus was like when he was the same age as _____. I wonder if he enjoyed building models like _____ does, or if he loved dancing like _____ does. (*Name some of the younger members of your group here.*)

We have just one story about Jesus when he was a child. This story happened when he was twelve years old, just like _____ here. (*Invite your twelve-year-old to the front.*) In this story, Jesus went on a long journey with his parents to join a celebration. Have you ever been on a long journey, _____ ? (*Invite your twelve-year-old to share their story, before asking your volunteers to be seated once again.*)

Jesus was twelve years old when his parents took him with them to Jerusalem to celebrate the Passover feast. The Passover was a big festival that God's people celebrated to remember God using Moses to save them from slavery in Egypt many, many years before.

Now remember, this was a long time ago, before the invention of cars, coaches or trains. Jesus and his parents had to walk all the way to Jerusalem. It would have taken them several days to get there, walking by day and setting up their tents by the roadside every night. It wasn't just Jesus and his parents taking the journey. All their friends and family travelled with them, all excited about the big celebration they would enjoy. I wonder what they talked about as they walked. I wonder how long they walked for each day. I wonder how long it was before Jesus said, 'Are we nearly there yet?'

Actually, the Bible doesn't say much about the journey to Jerusalem or even about the celebration itself. But when the time came to journey home, something very interesting happened.

When the Passover celebrations were over, Mary and Joseph packed up their bags and set off for home. They could see the

Session material: January
Where I belong by Becky May

children further up in front, chattering away about all the things they had seen and done during this Passover party; Jesus must be there with them, they thought. Mary and Joseph walked behind with the other adults, chatting and sharing their hopes for the journey home. It was like one massive family party. At the end of the first day, Mary and Joseph found a place to set up their camp and Mary went to find Jesus, but he wasn't there. He wasn't with the other children. In fact, nobody had seen him all day.

Poor Mary and Joseph – they had the most worrying time trying to find Jesus. They had to walk all the way back to Jerusalem and search high and low through the city. It actually took them three whole days to find Jesus!

When they did find Jesus, Mary and Joseph were very surprised about where he was. It was probably the last place you might expect to find a twelve-year-old boy: sitting in the temple with the temple leaders. The temple leaders were pretty surprised by Jesus too. He had been asking the most wonderful questions about God and he'd got them all thinking about a few things too. Then Jesus surprised everyone when he said, 'Didn't you know I'd be here in my Father's house?'

You see, Jesus knew that, just as he had been placed into a family and a community here on earth, he belonged to Father God. The great surprise for us is that Father God welcomes us into his family too.

8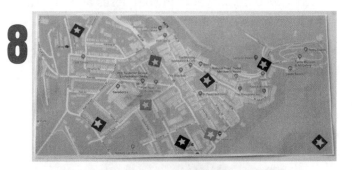

9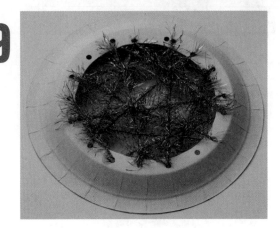

Prayer

Father God, thank you for our families and for our community here on earth. Thank you that we can be part of your family and we can call you our Dad. Amen

Song suggestions

'Hello, welcome' – Andy Pickford
'One family' – Pete James and Harvey Jessop
'We are one, we are family together' – Ishmael

Meal suggestion

A simple chicken casserole and meringue (popular Passover meals).

Session material: February
Self-confidence by Jen Robertson

 Go to messychurch.org.uk/ getmessyjan19 to download all templates at A4 size, including a session planning sheet

#discipleship: individual

Messy reflection by Becky May

The angel of the Lord came and sat down under the oak in Ophrah that belonged to Joash the Abiezrite, where his son Gideon was threshing wheat in a winepress to keep it from the Midianites. When the angel of the Lord appeared to Gideon, he said, 'The Lord is with you, mighty warrior.'

'Pardon me, my lord,' Gideon replied, 'but if the Lord is with us, why has all this happened to us? Where are all his wonders that our ancestors told us about when they said, "Did not the Lord bring us up out of Egypt?" But now the Lord has abandoned us and given us into the hand of Midian.'

The Lord turned to him and said, 'Go in the strength you have and save Israel out of Midian's hand. Am I not sending you?'

'Pardon me, my lord,' Gideon replied, 'but how can I save Israel? My clan is the weakest in Manasseh, and I am the least in my family.'

The Lord answered, 'I will be with you, and you will strike down all the Midianites, leaving none alive.'
Judges 6:11–16 (NIV)

If the doubting label had not been reserved for Thomas, perhaps we could have used it here for Gideon. 'I can't', 'I'm not', 'I'm only', 'We can't…' In this whole chapter, Gideon may well express himself as the most self-doubting character in the whole Bible! Moreover, Gideon expressed doubt in what God could do for him, looking for constant reassurances and proof that what God had said would indeed be true.

And every time Gideon expresses his doubt, God responds with reassurances of who he is and what he can do through Gideon. Every time, God is true to his word, doing all that he promises and demonstrating his power and authority.

Louie Giglio, an American pastor, once wrote of this interaction between man and God: 'I am not, but I know I AM.'

With us, as it was with Gideon, for all that we are not, cannot or have not, we are held in the hand of the one who is. Almighty God enabled Gideon to complete every task he called him to and will do the same for us today. Our self-confidence is not found in self-motivational books or inspirational fridge magnets, nor is it held in the record of our past achievements or the lack thereof.

When God calls us out of our comfort zones, we know he has gone before us. When he calls us to speak to someone for him, we know he prepares the way. When God places a desire or idea in our hearts, we know he has already equipped us with the gifts and skills we will need along the way.

Our almighty God did not need Gideon to work with him, but he chose to partner with Gideon, reminding us that God sees something special in each of us. Do we hear God whisper that to us today?

#discipleship: team

Messy health check

What part of doing Messy Church does each team member feel least confident about? How might you build each other up?

Messy team theme

- Have you ever felt like Gideon did at the start of the story?
- Which of the words that the angel brings to Gideon mean the most to you just now?
- What things in our world today are like the Asherah poles that God asked Gideon to remove?

How does this session help people grow in Christ?

This session helps us to think about our fears and our feelings about ourselves and to consider how God's words – his peace, his love and his encouragement – can speak into our lives and make a difference: bringing peace where there is fear, bringing courage where there is low self-esteem, bringing strength when we are weak. Gideon thought he was incapable and of no significance but, as he got to know God better, including being able to tell him exactly how he felt, his life changed forever. This session gives us that chance to come closer to God and to hear him speak to us in all our life situations, including nursery, school, work, community and home.

Session material: February

#discipleship: families

Mealtime card

- What three words would you use to describe yourself?
- If an angel appeared to you and described you, what three words would you like them to use?
- What difference does it make to know that God thinks you are incredible?

Take-home idea

Give each family an empty test tube which they should fill with water and add a few drops of food colouring to (have a variety to choose from). Put the stopper on and let them take it home, along with a single cheap white flower, for example a chrysanthemum or carnation. When they get home, they can put the flower in the test tube and watch the flower change colour as it absorbs the water over the next week. As you watch, remember that God can change us; we can receive his courage and strength, just like Gideon, when we feel weak and scared.

Question to start and end the session

So… how do you think of yourself? Brave and mighty or scared and weak?

#discipleship: extra

Get together and retell the story of Gideon and do just one activity together.

Activities

1. Shake it off

You will need: empty tissue boxes; wide ribbon or adjustable belt; six to eight table tennis balls; timer

Cut two slits into the bottom of the empty box of tissues and thread the wide ribbon or adjustable belt through the two slits to make a 'tissue box on a belt'! Remove the thin plastic barrier from the tissue box opening to make the game easier or keep it in place for a challenge! To play the game, strap the tissue box on to the player's back, and fill it with six to eight table tennis balls – then the player should shake, shimmy, jump and dance around to try to get the balls out of the tissue box. No using hands and no lying down! How many balls can people get rid of in a minute?

Talk about how Gideon was doing something nearly as ridiculous as this game at the start of today's story. He was trying to thresh wheat in a winepress, which was a big hole in the ground! You need to thresh wheat on a hilltop to let the wind blow away the chaff and keep the seeds for making into nice things like bread. It was a silly and embarrassing thing to do, and it showed how scared Gideon was. What kind of things make us scared and hide away?

2. God can help

You will need: glass tumblers; index cards; jug of water; basin

Fill the glass up with water (about half or two-thirds full). Place the index card over the top of the glass, ensuring that the whole of the rim is covered by it, and press down hard. Carefully flip the glass upside down, making sure you keep holding the card in place. You may get a few drips at this point, but don't panic! Slowly remove the hand holding the card out from underneath and the card should stick, holding the water at bay. It is probably sensible to have a basin underneath the glass when you do this. (You can also find this activity in *Messy Church Does Science* (BRF, 2017), p. 65.)

Talk about the fact that what is holding the card in place is the air pressure pressing upwards (stronger than gravity pressing downwards). We can't see the air pressure, but we know it must be working or the water would drop out. We know that God is there, holding us up and supporting us, just as he did for Gideon. God believed in Gideon even though Gideon didn't believe in himself. What things do you need to trust God for just now? How could doing so help you be more confident?

Self-confidence by Jen Robertson

3. Where is Gideon hiding?

You will need: nine people-shaped cards hidden around your Messy Church – each person-shaped piece should have one of the following words written on it: 'The Lord is with you, brave and mighty man' (Judges 6:12, GNT); scavenger hunt sheets to fill in (download online); pens

Hunt for the Gideons who are hidden around the room. Each Gideon has a word on it. Note each word as you find it and, when you have found all the words, make them into a sentence from today's story.

Talk about how Gideon was very scared. He thought he was too young and not important enough, but God called him a 'brave and mighty man'. What things do we think we are not good enough for? What things scare us? God is with us and knows how brilliant we really are even when we don't see it.

4. You are amazing!

You will need: white paper; paint; masking tape; permanent pens; Bibles or copies of today's story

Stick your tape across the paper in a criss-cross pattern. Paint over the whole piece of paper. This can be one colour or you can splatter paint across it. Carefully peel off the tape. Find the words from today's Bible story that are words of encouragement from God and write them in the blank spaces: for example, 'The Lord is with you', 'Mighty warrior', 'Go in the strength you have', 'I am sending you', 'I will be with you'.

Talk about how you feel about yourself. What words would you like to hear from God that would make you feel better about yourself?

5. Build an altar to the Lord

You will need: Lego; blindfolds

Build an altar using Lego, but do it blindfolded!

Talk about how easy or difficult you found it to build the altar with the Lego while blindfolded. In Gideon's day, people built altars to God, places where they could show God that they loved him and he was the most important thing in their lives. In Gideon's town, everyone had stopped doing this and had built statues to other gods. Gideon wanted to build an altar, but he did it at night-time because he was worried that people would see him and kill him for building it. Do you like telling people that you love God? Are you sometimes scared about what people might think?

6. A fire on a rock

You will need: paper plates; digestive biscuits; chocolate icing; red and orange jelly sweets; chocolate fingers; chocolate flakes; knives or spoons (to spread the icing)

Cover your digestive biscuit with chocolate icing and put the coloured sweets on top of the icing. Break the chocolate fingers in half and place over the sweets to make the logs of the fire. Sprinkle some flakes on top to look like kindling.

Talk about how Gideon asked God to show him that he really was God. Gideon brought out some meat and bread to the angel and put it on a rock. When the angel touched it with a stick, it all burned up. What would you like God to do to show you that he really is God?

7. Peace, don't be afraid

You will need: individual canvases or one large canvas to work on together; old newspapers; Decopatch glue (Mod Podge); paintbrushes; black paint; black sharpies; scissors

Rip or cut out stories/images of conflict from the newspapers and glue them on to the canvas, then cover the newspaper with a top coat of the glue. Once the canvas is covered with the newspaper cuttings and the glue is dry, write/paint across the paper the words 'Peace, don't be afraid'. Bring the one large canvas or individual canvases to the celebration.

Talk about how Gideon's fear and his belief that he was too insignificant had eroded his self-confidence, but God speaks into all his feelings and gives him peace: peace to be himself, peace to do things he had never imagined he could, peace to follow God's ways. What difference would it make to you today to hear God say, 'Peace, do not be afraid', in our world, amid our own problems?

8. Blindfolded obstacle course

You will need: objects to create an obstacle course, e.g. crash mats, chairs, tables, hoops; blindfolds

Build an obstacle course. People need to navigate the course in pairs, one blindfolded and the other acting as their guide to ensure they make their way to the end safely. Swap round so everybody has a turn at both roles.

Talk about how the person who was blindfolded felt. Did they trust their partner? What did their partner do that helped? What was the most difficult part? Gideon didn't know where he was going; he needed to trust God to show him the way ahead. What kind of things do we need to trust God for today?

Session material: February

9. Parachutes

You will need: square-shaped pieces of material; string; large buttons with four holes; fabric pens; sticky tape; scissors

Cut four equal pieces of string per parachute, about 45–60 cm in length. Thread each string through a separate hole in the button, then tie them together, leaving a few centimetres trailing at the bottom. Lay out your cloth and tape one string to each corner of the material. Write on the cloth, 'Go in the strength you have.'

Stand at the top of some stairs or go somewhere high like the pulpit. Pray for God to give you the strength to rely on him, whatever you are doing. Release the parachute as a sign of entrusting your prayer to God.

Talk about how, as Gideon got to know God better, he realised he could trust him, which made him braver and stronger. How can we get to know God better?

10. Doves of peace

You will need: paper squares; printed instructions on how to make a dove of peace (download online); pens

Write some things that you are worried about or frightened of on the square, and then write 'You can do it because I will help you' on the other side. Then follow the instructions to fold the paper into a dove of peace. Bring your dove with you to the celebration.

Talk about how God transformed Gideon's life. He was scared, in hiding and lacking in confidence, but then he met with God and things looked totally different. What part of your life would you like God to change?

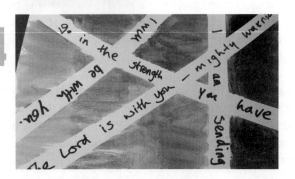

Celebration

You will need: a large parachute (or some blankets if you don't have room); peace canvas(es) from activity 7; doves of peace from activity 10

During the activities, give out the following words to one or more of the congregation explaining that they will be the angel in the story during the celebration, and will need to say these words in a loud and confident voice when you say, 'The angel said...' (If you choose more than one person, make sure they all know which number they are).

1. 'The Lord is with you, brave and mighty man' (Judges 6:12, GNT).
2. 'Go with all your great strength and rescue the Israelites. I myself am sending you' (Judges 6:14, GNT).
3. 'You can do it because I will help you' (Judges 6:16, GNT).
4. 'Peace, don't be afraid' (Judges 6:23, GNT).

Gather everyone round a parachute. While they are holding the parachute, get everyone to take a step into the middle, then lift the parachute over their heads and bring it down under their bottoms so they are sitting on the edge of the parachute, forming a large tent. Invite one person to stand in the middle of the dome to raise the roof slightly, to make it more like a big top.

Once everyone is safely inside the 'tent', explain that today's story starts with all the people of God, the Israelites, hiding – hiding from the very strong and powerful Midianites and Amalekites. They hid in caves and other safe places. They were terrified. The Midianites and the Amalekites had huge armies, and so many camels that you couldn't count them. They stole all the Israelites' animals and food and destroyed their homes. All the Israelites shouted out to God for help. (*Get everyone to shout together: 'God help us! God help us!'*) God listened and sent help. (*Invite everyone to come out from under the parachute and sit back in their 'normal' seats.*) Here is how God helped: he sent an angel to speak to a man called Gideon.

(*Invite someone to be Gideon to help with the dramatisation of the story, asking them to spontaneously respond in mime to what you read out. You may need to give them some direction and help with this.*)

Gideon was scared.
Gideon was worried.
He was hiding.
He was trying to thresh some wheat.
It wasn't working.
There was no wind to help.

Suddenly an angel appeared.
The angel said... (1) 'The Lord is with you, brave and mighty man.'

Self-confidence by Jen Robertson

Gideon was shocked.
Gideon was amused.
Gideon was angry.
Gideon said, 'God has abandoned us!'

The angel said... (2) 'Go with all your great strength
and rescue the Israelites. I myself am sending you.'

Gideon said, 'I can't do that.
I come from a weak clan
and I am the least important member of my family!'

The angel said... (3) 'You can do it because I will help you.'
Gideon said, 'Show me proof that you really are God!'
Gideon brought the angel some bread, soup
and meat and put it on a rock.
The angel touched it with a stick
and it burst into flames.
Then the angel disappeared, just like that!
Gideon knew he had really met with God.

Later on, the angel said... (4) 'Peace, don't be afraid.'
And then asked him
to go and knock down all the statues
that all his neighbours had built to worship other gods,
not the one true God.

Gideon took ten people with him
and knocked down all the statues
during the night.
It was too scary a thing to do during the day!
Then he built an altar to God.
The whole town was raging.

(*Get the whole congregation to shout at Gideon.*)

Gideon's dad came out
and spoke to them all.
He said that the other gods
could deal with Gideon
if they had a problem
with him knocking down their statues.
And everyone was happy
with that plan.

They followed Gideon.
Gideon knew God was with him.
Gideon blew a trumpet.
Gideon was in charge.
Gideon led the people out
to defend Israel.

Gideon was brave.
Gideon was strong.
Gideon knew God was with him.

Prayer

Look together at the peace canvas(es) with the words 'Peace, do not be afraid' written on them. Invite everyone to be silent for a moment (around 20 seconds) and to think about something in their life that needs God's peace. Once the time is up, play a piece of quiet worship music and invite everyone to lay their doves of peace around the picture. Then pray this prayer together:

Lord, we often feel scared and inadequate, like Gideon. Help us to hear you speaking to us: 'Peace, do not be afraid.' Amen

Song suggestions

'Build your kingdom here' – Rend Collective
'Our God' – Chris Tomlin
'Lord, I need you' – Matt Maher
'Your grace is enough' – Matt Maher
'Never give up' – Hillsong Kids
'I am loved' – Heather Price

Meal suggestion

If the weather permits, have a BBQ with meat and bread. If not, burgers, salad and all the trimmings inside is just as good, with ice-cream cones for pudding.

6

7

9

10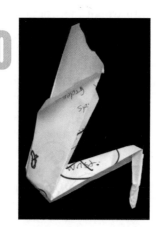

Session material: March

 Go to **messychurch.org.uk/ getmessyjan19** to download all templates at A4 size, including a session planning sheet

#discipleship: individual

Messy reflection by Greg Ross

But Jesus went to the Mount of Olives. At dawn he appeared again in the temple courts, where all the people gathered round him, and he sat down to teach them. The teachers of the law and the Pharisees brought in a woman caught in adultery. They made her stand before the group and said to Jesus, 'Teacher, this woman was caught in the act of adultery. In the Law Moses commanded us to stone such women. Now what do you say?' They were using this question as a trap, in order to have a basis for accusing him.

But Jesus bent down and started to write on the ground with his finger. When they kept on questioning him, he straightened up and said to them, 'Let any one of you who is without sin be the first to throw a stone at her.' Again he stooped down and wrote on the ground.

At this, those who heard began to go away one at a time, the older ones first, until only Jesus was left, with the woman still standing there. Jesus straightened up and asked her, 'Woman, where are they? Has no one condemned you?'

'No one, sir,' she said.

'Then neither do I condemn you,' Jesus declared. 'Go now and leave your life of sin.'

John 8:1–11 (NIV)

At first reading, this story may seem to be about someone breaking their marriage vows. Interestingly, the other person with whom the woman was caught is not brought before Jesus, so we only have one half of the couple being accused.

Rather than focusing on the woman and her actions, Jesus turns his attention to those who have so proudly brought this 'sinner' to public view. We have no idea what Jesus wrote in the dirt. While it might be fascinating to try to speculate, it would take away from the central focus of Jesus' active message.

By his action, Jesus demonstrated that this woman whom others had named as a 'sinner' was as much a person of worth as those who accused her. And Jesus goes further by demonstrating that he was someone who would accept her and not judge her.

Jesus' desire for all people is for each one, no matter their station in life, their background or anything, to live abundantly as people of worth. Each one is a daughter or son of God; each one is created in the image of God. By lifting up the woman as a person of worth and not focusing on her past action, Jesus was pointing to the power and wonder of forgiveness and grace. People's pasts do not have to dictate their whole future. Change and transformation are possible.

Each person has a responsibility to live as a daughter or son of God and to treat every other person with the same respect. This is really hard and requires discipline and practice. The old Jewish understanding of 'sin' was 'not to live up to the potential for which you were created by God'. Living up to our potential in Christ, and enabling others to work towards becoming more and more like Jesus, is the aim or target of our lives and ministry. For me, this lifelong goal is possible only through the ongoing work of the Spirit in my life. I hope it is the same for you.

#discipleship: team

Messy health check

Has your team developed any bad habits that you need to recognise before Jesus and receive forgiveness for?

Messy team theme

- What makes Jesus 'break the rules'?
- How does Jesus make people feel?
- How can you show kindness to people at Messy Church?

How does this session help people grow in Christ?

In today's Messy Church, we explore the theme of kindness and friendship as we look at the story of the woman who is brought before the crowd to be stoned to death. There are three important aspects of the story:
- Jesus isn't afraid to go against the socially expected norm, when he befriends the woman who is caught in this messy situation.
- Jesus puts a new lens on the situation that shifts people's perceptions.
- Jesus sets the woman free for a fresh start – a different life to the one she was leading.

As we work through the aspects of the story, we discover how Jesus changes the world (including us) one person at a time.

❖ @MessyChurchBRF

Dusty drawing by Jean Pienaar

Using Christ's example of kindness and friendship, we can reach out to the marginalised and be part of making the world a better place.

#discipleship: families

Mealtime card

- Who is your best friend?
- Who is the kindest person that you know?
- How can you be kind to others at Messy Church?

Take-home idea

Think of someone in your neighbourhood who needs a little gesture of kindness. What can you do to show them that Jesus cares about them? Perhaps you can make and drop off a card or some homemade cookies, or even just give them a smile. Challenge your family to complete one random act of kindness each week.

Lord Jesus, you reached out to the woman in her mess and distress, with words of kindness and not condemnation. Help us to reach out to people around us with your gift of love, as together we can change the world one person at a time. Amen

Question to start and end the session

So… who does Jesus want us to reach out to?

#discipleship: extra

Go for a walk and find somewhere to draw on the ground with sand, mud, chalk or whatever doesn't harm the environment, and remind everyone of this story.

1

Activities

1. Friendship bracelet

You will need: seven lengths of embroidery thread or wool (50 cm in length) per person; cardboard discs (cereal-box thickness); scissors; pens

Divide the cardboard disc into eight 'slices' by drawing four lines (like a pizza). Make a hole in the middle of the cardboard disc. Cut slits – about 1.5 cm on each line – from the outside of the circle. Tie the seven threads together using an overhand knot. Pull the threads through the centre hole so that the knot is on the other (back) side, and the seven loose threads are towards you. Put the individual pieces of wool into seven of the slits. Turn the disc so that the empty slit is facing down. Count three slits to the left of the empty slit and move the wool from there to the empty slit. Turn the disc so that the new empty slit is at the bottom and repeat the process: count three slits to the left and move that piece of wool to the empty slit at the bottom. Over time, the length of the knotted friendship bracelet will grow out the back. When you have completed sufficient length, tie another overhand knot to secure the knotting you have completed. Leave a little gap and tie another overhand knot (forming a 'buttonhole'). Trim the ends with scissors. Thread the beginning knot through the buttonhole to secure the friendship bracelet. (See video online for visual instructions.) Give the bracelet to a true friend.

This can take a long time, so if people get bored they can stop knotting when it's too short to be a bracelet and take it home as it is – or leave for the next person to complete.

Talk about the friends you have. What makes a true friend? How can you be a friend to those you meet? How is Jesus your friend?

2. Painting stones

You will need: small smooth stones or pebbles; aprons; acrylic paints; paintbrushes; containers for water to rinse brushes; aerosol varnish (optional); plant pot

Use acrylic paints to decorate smooth pebbles. Leave these to dry and then varnish (in a well-ventilated space) if desired. Place the painted stone gently in a plant pot.

Talk about how we can change potentially damaging objects into objects of beauty. Think about the words we use when we speak to others – do they hurt or heal? How did Jesus interact with the woman who was brought before him?

Session material: March

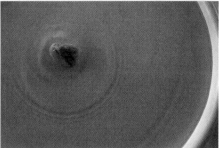

3. Second-chance craft

You will need: empty tin cans (make sure the exposed edge is not too sharp); hammer; nails (of different thicknesses); long-nose pliers; wire; heart outlines; Blu Tack (to hold outline in place) or permanent marker; spray paint (optional); tealight candle or electric tealight

Fill the empty cans with water and leave in the freezer overnight so they don't buckle when you punch the nails in.

Position the heart outline on the side of the can with Blu Tack or draw around it with a permanent marker. Use the hammer and nails (ensure adult supervision of younger people) to outline the shape. Long-nose pliers can be used to hold the nails in place as you go. Make two additional holes near the upper rim and thread some wire for a handle. On completing the holes, leave the can in the sun so that the water melts, or soak it in warm water to speed up the process. If the bottom of the can has bulged with the ice, bash it inwards once the ice has melted. When the can is fully dry, spray paint, if desired. Place a tealight candle in the bottom of the can.

Talk about how recycling gives unwanted items another chance. How did Jesus give the woman in the story another chance? How do you think that made the woman feel?

4. Ripple effect

You will need: basin or tray filled with water (a wide, shallow surface of water is best); small objects of different weights and sizes (e.g. marble, coin, paperclip, grain of sand)

Place the tray of water on the ground (or on a sturdy table). Starting with the larger objects and working towards the smaller objects, see which of these items cause a ripple effect in the water. Watch carefully.

Talk about how the things we do and say cause ripples in other people's lives. Is it just the big things that cause ripples, or can small things also cause the water to ripple? How important is it that we create ripples of kindness?

5. Paperchain of friendship

You will need: A4 sheets of paper; scissors; coloured pens

Fold the A4 sheet in half (from top to bottom) and then in half again, so that the original width of the A4 sheet is still available. Turn the folded paper so that it is tall and thin rather than short and wide. On the top column of paper, draw an outline of a person so that the arms and feet go right to the

Dusty drawing by Jean Pienaar

edge. Cut out the person shape so that the result is four people with their hands and feet joined. Think of four different ways to be kind and write each of these ideas on a paper person. You may like to display these.

Talk about different ways of being kind and how to be a good friend.

6. Sponge shot

You will need: small sponges (or paper scrunched into balls); cardboard target (or bucket lid)

If you are feeling brave and the weather is suitable, take this activity outside and add some water! Challenge the participants to take aim and throw the sponges at the target. If you have a willing volunteer, have them stand in as the target.

Talk about what it feels like to throw the sponges and hit the target. Also talk about what it feels like to be the target. What is the difference between throwing sponges and throwing stones?

7. Sand writing

You will need: tray(s) with a thin layer of sand

Set up this activity in a quiet corner. Use your fingers to draw or write a message in the sand.

Talk about what Jesus might have written in the sand, and what message you might want to write to Jesus. Shake the tray when you have finished so that someone else can have a turn.

8. Emoji biscuits

You will need: round biscuits; yellow icing; black icing pens; small sweets (e.g. Smarties); print-out of different emojis; plates; spoons for the icing

Choose an emoji that represents one of the emotions of the characters in the story, for example anger, worry or sadness. Ice the biscuit with yellow icing and suitable decorations.

Talk about the emoji you have chosen. Who does it represent in the story? When have you ever felt like this?

9. Sandwich bank

You will need: bread; margarine; various sandwich fillings; knives; chopping board; containers

Make sandwiches to distribute (after Messy Church) to people in need – possibly a local shelter or health clinic (check the

need beforehand). If this is not possible where you are, make something less perishable (for example, fill and decorate a bag of sweets) to give out somewhere in the coming week.

Talk about what it means to show friendship to a stranger. How do you think the accused woman felt when Jesus talked to her and showed compassion?

10. Building bridges

You will need: drinking straws (preferably non-bending); scissors; masking tape; two bricks (or piles of books) about 35 cm apart; small polystyrene trays; coins, stones or weights

Using the drinking straws and tape, design and construct a bridge that will span a length of 35 cm and carry as much weight as possible. Place a polystyrene tray on the bridge and see how many coins it can hold before it collapses.

Talk about how Jesus showed kindness by reaching out to a stranger. By building bridges and finding common ground, we are able to reach out to strangers and share God's love with them. What are the ways in which we can reach out to others and 'build bridges'?

8

9

10

Session material: March
Dusty drawing by Jean Pienaar

Celebration

You will need: picture of a single person on one end of the paper and a crowd of people on the other side, with two arrows pointing at the single person (download online); glass jug filled with water

In today's story, we have a much more serious version of playground tittle-tattle: running off to the teacher to report the misdemeanour. But it's not just one person who has noticed that the woman did something wrong; it's a whole group of Pharisees and teachers of the law – learned men who were trying to uphold the law and preserve Jewish tradition – who are waiting to see how Jesus responds.

We aren't told if Jesus listened to both sides of the story, but he certainly doesn't give an immediate judgement. Jesus writes something in the dirt on the ground.

The scene must look a bit like this picture – a whole group of people pointing fingers at one person, the woman who was caught in adultery. She must be very worried about what is going to happen next.

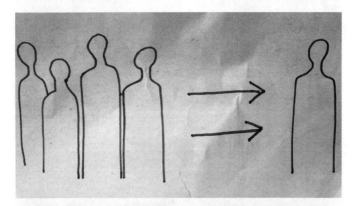

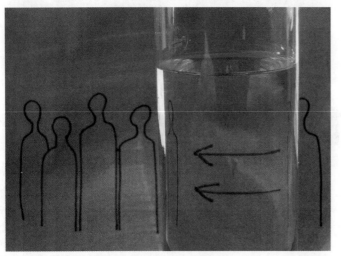

When Jesus does speak, he tells the people gathered that if any of them are without sin, they can throw the first stone. Jesus comes with a new lens. (*Place jug of water in front of the arrows.*) Where are the arrows pointing now?

The fingers are now pointing to the crowd of people! And they all start to leave as they realise that they have also sinned.

Eventually, Jesus is left alone with the woman. He asks whether anyone has judged her. On hearing that no one has judged her, he tells her that neither does he judge her. Jesus tells her to go and sin no more.

I wonder… which part of the story you like best.

I wonder… which part is the most important.

I wonder… where you are in the story or what part of the story is about you.

Prayer

Use your finger (only!) to write or draw on the floor, as you think of things you are sorry for.

Use your finger to point to someone who has been kind to you and thank Jesus for that person and their kindness.

Use your finger to draw a heart on your hand and think about how you can be kind to someone else. Ask Jesus to be with you as you reach out to them.

Song suggestions

'In a deep, deep place' – Fischy Music
'Tell the world' – Hillsong Kids
'He's got the whole world in his hands' – traditional
'Jesus' hands were kind hands' – Frank McConnell

Meal suggestion

(Remember to get people to wash their hands after writing on the floor with their fingers!) Wraps using tomato, lettuce, cucumber, cooked chicken and sauces such as mayonnaise or sweet chilli (wrapping up goodness and kindness). Seasonal fruit for dessert.

Session material: April
Always with us by Greg Ross

 Go to messychurch.org.uk/ getmessyjan19 to download all templates at A4 size, including a session planning sheet

#discipleship: individual

Messy reflection by Jen Robertson

When Pilate saw that it was no use to go on, but that a riot might break out, he took some water, washed his hands in front of the crowd, and said, 'I am not responsible for the death of this man! This is your doing!' The whole crowd answered, 'Let the responsibility for his death fall on us and on our children!' Then Pilate set Barabbas free for them; and after he had Jesus whipped, he handed him over to be crucified...

At noon the whole country was covered with darkness, which lasted for three hours. At about three o'clock Jesus cried out with a loud shout, *'Eli, Eli, lema sabachthani?'* which means, 'My God, my God, why did you abandon me?'... Jesus again gave a loud cry and breathed his last... There were many women there, looking on from a distance, who had followed Jesus from Galilee and helped him. Among them were Mary Magdalene, Mary the mother of James and Joseph, and the wife of Zebedee.

When it was evening, a rich man from Arimathea arrived; his name was Joseph, and he also was a disciple of Jesus. He went into the presence of Pilate and asked for the body of Jesus. Pilate gave orders for the body to be given to Joseph. So Joseph took it, wrapped it in a new linen sheet, and placed it in his own tomb, which he had just recently dug out of solid rock. Then he rolled a large stone across the entrance to the tomb and went away. Mary Magdalene and the other Mary were sitting there, facing the tomb...

After the Sabbath, as Sunday morning was dawning, Mary Magdalene and the other Mary went to look at the tomb. Suddenly there was a violent earthquake; an angel of the Lord came down from heaven, rolled the stone away, and sat on it. His appearance was like lightning, and his clothes were white as snow. The guards were so afraid that they trembled and became like dead men.

The angel spoke to the women. 'You must not be afraid,' he said. 'I know you are looking for Jesus, who was crucified. He is not here; he has been raised, just as he said. Come here and see the place where he was lying. Go quickly now, and tell his disciples, "He has been raised from death, and now he is going to Galilee ahead of you; there you will see him!" Remember what I have told you.'

So they left the tomb in a hurry, afraid and yet filled with joy, and ran to tell his disciples.
Matthew 27—28 (GNT, abridged)

Matthew's detailed narrative, deeply rooted in Jewish culture and tradition, comes to its dramatic, ugly and brutal climax in these two chapters. As the number of characters increases in this story of plots and counter-plots, the central character of Jesus says very little as he is questioned, beaten, bullied and abused. All around him is noise and brutality: crowds shouting and demanding, leaders manipulating and denying their responsibilities, friends running away.

Interestingly, Matthew notes how the women in the story remain faithful and sincere: Pilate's wife sends a message to her husband to leave Jesus alone due to his innocence; the women stay and watch at the cross; the two Marys watch Joseph of Arimathea as he and his friends seal the tomb shut, and return on that glorious morning two days later.

Jesus' silence is broken dramatically when he shouts out at about three o'clock, 'My God, my God, why did you abandon me?' Jesus is obviously in deep anguish. But the amazing news is that he did this even for the religious leaders who plotted for his death; for Pilate who represents the most powerful man in the world, the emperor; for Judas who betrayed him; for Barabbas who had been set free in his place – and for me and for you.

#discipleship: team

Messy health check

What does Jesus' cross mean to each person in your team?

Messy team theme

- How can we best share the wondrous news that Easter is all about the new life that the love of God brings to us in Christ?
- How do we make a space for people to ask questions?
- How do we enable and support them as they discover and respond to God's love themselves?

Session material: April

How does this session help people grow in Christ?

Easter is the central and most important event of the Christian faith. Each time we tell the story and invite people to enter into the story, there is always a new truth or something deeper to discover, or another perspective that is opened.

#discipleship: families

Mealtime card

- What part of the Easter story do you like the best?
- When do you feel that God is closest to you?
- Is there any part of the Easter story that we could leave out and still have a complete narrative?

Take-home idea

Make your own Easter scene with figures for the different parts of the story. These can be as simple as a series of seven pictures that are hand-drawn, coloured in or taken from books, to peg figures, clay/Fimo figures or hand-carved figures, to making your own 'stop-motion' movies on your computer.

Creator God, thank you so much for Easter and for Jesus, who has shown us that nothing can stop you loving us. Thank you that you never leave us, even though we sometimes might feel like we are alone. May your Holy Spirit strengthen us to choose to follow Jesus' way, even when it is hard. Amen

Question to start and end the session

So… what in the story of Easter is most important to you?

#discipleship: extra

Have a safari meal around three or four different houses during the Easter holiday.

Activities

1. Create your own 'Stations of the Cross'

You will need: list of Stations of the Cross (traditional or scriptural); various dressing-up clothes and props; camera; printer (optional)

Look at the list of the traditional or scriptural Stations of the Cross – the story of Jesus' journey towards the cross. Using the dressing-up clothes and props, recreate one or more of the stations and take a picture. Have an instant camera available, or the means to connect the camera to a printer. You might like to have somewhere to display the photos, so that people can see what other groups have done. If this is not possible, keep the photos for use in the future (ensuring you have the relevant permissions).

Talk about what Jesus' journey to the cross might have been like. How did you feel when recreating these scenes? Which Station of the Cross speaks most to you? Why?

2. Easter story scene

You will need: modelling clay, playdough or Fimo clay

Invite people to allow their fingers to guide them as they make a series of figures that can be taken home to remind them of the whole or their favourite part of the Easter story.

Talk about whether anyone has a favourite toy, book or other possession that they take with them to most places. What does that particular thing help them remember, or make them feel? Do you have ways or objects that help you remember the Easter story?

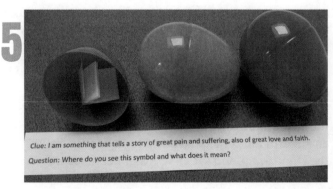

Clue: I am something that tells a story of great pain and suffering, also of great love and faith.

Question: Where do you see this symbol and what does it mean?

Always with us by Greg Ross

3. Write your own Easter story song

You will need: paper; pens; instruments such as a guitar, keyboard or xylophone (optional)

Write your own version of the Easter story in a song. How well can you retell the story? If you don't want to come up with your own tune, use a traditional one such as 'Amazing Grace'. If you like, use the instruments to accompany your song. You could do this in pairs, small groups or individually. Here are two verses (to the tune of 'Amazing Grace') that you could use as an example:

Long time ago, so far away,
a man named Jesus lived,
he showed us how to live God's dream
and welcome everyone.

Jerusalem was where he came
to teach and heal and love.
The crowds all waved and welcomed him
but that was soon to change.

Talk about your favourite Easter song.

4. 'What Easter means to me' video

You will need: mobile phone or camera to record video; video projector (optional)

Set up a station in one corner or room of the building where there is not as much background noise and invite families or groups of people in twos or threes to come and tell what the Easter story is about for them. If you have the facilities, you could show this during the celebration or, if you have the relevent permission, post it on your Messy Church Facebook page.

Talk about whether you tell your friends and family that you come to Messy Church and that you choose to follow the way of Jesus. Is telling people easy or difficult? What is the most important message that the Easter story teaches us?

5. Easter discovery hunt

You will need: hollow plastic eggs that can be opened; printed answer sheets (download online); pens

Prepare a series of questions and answers that will help participants discover how some of the 'things we take for granted' in church spaces remind us of the Easter story, e.g. the cross, stained-glass windows, tapestries, artworks, banners, etc. Then prepare a series of clues that will guide the participants to those particular items. Some examples can be downloaded online.

Type your questions on a sheet with spaces to write answers alongside and place the answers in the eggs and hide them in or near the objects you want them to find. This works well as an intergenerational and/or household activity.

Talk about how when we come to a building like a church we can see things we don't recognise and there may be things we do not notice. Messy Church is a time for discovering things about Jesus and for asking questions about God.

6. Messy hot cross scones or buns

You will need: ingredients and means to make and cook buns/scones (or premade buns/scones); edible decorations such as icing sugar, sweets, chocolate, etc.

Find a recipe for buns/scones that suits your Messy Church (be aware of allergies). You can find recipes here: **pinterest. co.uk/MessyChurchBRF/lent-easter**. If you have access to an oven, make the dough and cook it. If you have time after they have cooled, decorate at Messy Church or you can send them home to decorate. Alternatively, make or buy buns/scones beforehand and decorate at Messy Church, or simply make the dough at Messy Church and give everyone a piece to cook at home.

Talk about the way that hot cross buns or scones remind us of the story of Easter. What else reminds you of the Easter story?

7. Pallet cross

You will need: old wooden pallets, taken apart and nails removed; thick string or twine; hammer and nails or screws and screwdrivers; cardboard sign and marker pens (optional)

Using thick string or twine, invite participants to lash one long and one short piece of wood together to make a cross. (If you are short of time, you could have some premade and screwed together and then add the string or twine over the top.) Depending on the age of your participants, you may invite them to partially hammer a nail/screw into the places where Jesus' hands and feet would have been nailed. You may also have a cardboard sign for them to attach to the top. You could use the traditional 'King of the Jews' wording or something like 'Such love' or 'Amazing grace'.

Talk about how recycling the old pallet reminds us of the transformative power of God. Some of Jesus' friends were not considered very important (lepers, homeless people, children, widows) but Jesus' love changed them and they were able to direct people to Jesus. Wonder if or how the love of God has changed someone you know or the way you think about yourself or other people.

Session material: April

8. 'Christ is risen' wooden sign

You will need: leftover timber (perhaps from activity 7); drills and screws or nails and hammers, or strong wood glue; pencils; paint and paint brushes

Each person will need three pieces of timber – two wide, flat pieces which will become the sign itself, and one thinner and smaller piece to be the bracing across the back of the sign. If you have people with sufficient skill to manage the tools, drill and then nail the bracing to the back of your sign. Use thick card and strong glue if obtaining the wood is too difficult.

Have available templates or pictures of flowers that bloom around Easter time in your country. Encourage people to trace or copy a flower design on to their sign and then paint 'Christ is risen'.

Talk about how Jesus' resurrection and new life has brought people hope in the past and still brings people hope today.

9. Palm frond crosses

You will need: instructions for making palm frond crosses (easily found online, such as at wikihow. com/make-a-palm-frond-cross); large palm-like leaves

Show people how to cut and fold the frond into a cross that they can take home. Use this time to link the story of Palm Sunday with the story of the cross.

Talk about the way that the story of Jesus goes from a big welcome party on the day known as Palm Sunday to the sadness of Good Friday with Jesus being killed. How does the Easter story make you feel? Does it make a difference knowing that Jesus rose again?

10. The colours of Easter jewellery

You will need: string or plastic twine; colourful beads, including crosses; craft clips or clasps

Create a bracelet or string of beads with a range of colours that reminds you of the colours of the Easter story. For example, bright greens for Palm Sunday; red and brown for the wine and bread at the last supper; dark colours for Jesus' arrest, beating and death; black for Easter Saturday; and bright, joyful colours for Easter Sunday and the empty tomb.

Talk about what these colours remind you of. If people ask you what the colours on your jewellery mean, what will you say?

🇫 📌 🐦 **@MessyChurchBRF**

Always with us by Greg Ross

Celebration

Easter is a good time of year to celebrate Holy Communion together or, if you have anyone in your Messy congregation who wants to dedicate their life to Jesus, to have Messy baptisms. You may like to incorporate these into your celebration.

Invite people to be part of the very surprising resurrection or new life story. Think of a time when you were very sad and remember how that felt. Also remember a time when someone did or said something that helped you feel warm, loved and safe. Be ready to bring those feelings to different parts of this story.

Ask for some volunteers to help tell the story. You need two people to be guards, two to be the Marys, one to be the angel and one to be Jesus. Everyone else can join in with sound effects as needed.

A few days after Jesus had died, two of his friends, who were both called Mary, got up very early and went to the graveyard where Jesus was buried. (*Invite your audience to make sounds of footsteps.*)

His grave was being guarded by two soldiers. (*Soldiers stand around, looking fierce and on guard.*)

Suddenly an earthquake struck the area. (*Make earthquake sounds – crashing and banging. The Marys and guards scream in fear and fall to the ground.*)

When the shaking stopped, the two friends of Jesus who were both called Mary stood up and saw that the earthquake had caused the stone that sealed Jesus' grave to open. A bright, shiny being was sitting on the tomb stone. (*The Marys shake in fear as the angel comes on.*)

The angel told them: 'Do not be afraid, for God's love has raised Jesus to new life. You are to gather Jesus' friends and go from Jerusalem to meet him at his favourite getaway spot near the lake.'

The women ran to share the news with their friends. (*Make running sounds.*) Suddenly, on the road in front of them, they saw Jesus. They fell down and worshipped him. (*The Marys bow down.*)

Jesus spoke the same message as the angel: 'Do not be afraid, my friends. Go and tell my other friends that I will meet them at our favourite getaway spot near the lake!'

This is the very surprising good news of Easter: we do not need to be afraid of death. God's love is more powerful than anything. Jesus is alive!

Three cheers for God's love!

Hip hip – HOORAH!
Hip hip – HOORAH!
Hip hip – HOORAH!

If some of your teams wrote their own Easter story song, you could put the words on the screen and invite everyone to sing it together. If your 'What Easter means to me' video is ready to play, show this now or play it while people are sharing a meal.

Prayer

If you have an 'Easter scene' set up in your church space, you may choose to give everyone a stone to lay at the foot of the cross or at the empty tomb as a way of offering a thank-you prayer to God for taking away our fear of death and being alone.

Alternatively, you may like to create a cardboard cross and invite people to come and write their thank-you messages to God all around the cross – during a time in which there is some quiet music playing. This could also be done with Post-it notes or similar. Then you can share a prayer like this one together:

Loving God, we thank you for the great mystery of Easter. We know that Jesus was born in a country far from here, that he grew up and spent his life helping people and bringing them close to you. We are sad that he was killed. We are so glad that your love brought him back to new life and that he is no longer in one place, but now he is in every place and every time and always with us! For this amazing gift of love we shout our thanks together: THANK YOU, GOD, FOR JESUS! Amen

Song suggestions

'Hosanna rock' – Yancy
'Lord, I lift your name on high' – Rick Founds
'In the bulb there is a flower' – Natalie Sleeth
'Oi, oi, we are gonna praise the Lord' – Doug Horley
'I see God in you' – Heather Price

Meal suggestion

Your nation or region may have foods that are commonly served at Easter celebrations. Otherwise, choose anything that will help you have a celebratory meal: party foods, foods for special treats, foods that remind people of milestones and new beginnings.

Dear Jane

Advice for Messy Church leaders from Jane Leadbetter

✉ Email jane.leadbetter@brf.org.uk with your Messy questions and for advice.

Sandra in Birmingham

We are enjoying our Messy Church very much but how can we create real conversations when we are so busy preparing for and then doing the Messy Church sessions? How can we get to know the families better?

Hi Sandra

Thank you for all you are doing for the families in your community. Be excited about the opportunities you have! Conversations can take place during the whole two hours of a typical Messy Church: at the welcome table, over the activity areas, sharing the Bible story and at meal times. We have seen some great ideas. We love the 'Messy Chatterer' idea: find someone who is comfortable with talking to people who they may not know (this is not in everyone's comfort zone). Invite them to roam the Messy Church talking to all ages and recording any needs or prayer requests. In time, over the months, the families will come to expect this person to be the Messy Chatterer and be a key person to ask about anything, at each session. Make giveaway cards for new people and place them on the meal tables so that the Chatterer can be contacted at any time for prayer requests or info. You can learn a lot about the families, their issues and concerns, by reading their prayers.

In most of our resources, including this magazine, we offer table talk ideas to help with conversations over the activity areas. These could be prompt cards or included in the menu-style activity instructions that lots of Messy Churches use. Always include a 'talk about' sentence with open-ended questions, or use Godly Play style 'I wonder' questions where there are no right or wrong answers.

The conversations at the meal table can be prompted with a table talk time as well. During the first course of the meal, you can ask everyone to chat about what they have enjoyed the most from the Messy Church that day. Position team members on each table to develop conversations. The children don't hold back! Just go for it. During the cake or dessert time, ask an 'I wonder' question about something in the Bible story or theme of the month. You will hear real responses and it will give you constructive feedback regarding how well the celebration time went.

Keep records of what worked well in the celebration, and also what didn't work so well.

One of the best ways of getting to know the families is by going outdoors. We hear about so many special times, conversations and friendships that started when walking together along a stream or footpath, on a Messy Hike, at a Messy Camp or a Messy Picnic, for example. I surprised myself at my own Messy Church when I was talking to two members of my own Messy team during a Messy picnic. We discovered so much about each other, our hopes for the future and why Messy Church was so important in their lives. I had no idea about the power of a salmon sandwich outdoors!

June in Berkshire

Our Messy Church is three years old and mostly the same Messy roles are still covered by the same people. Do other churches work this way? I am wondering if things will fall apart if I try to change anything, yet I feel ready to invite the team to swap around a bit. But I am afraid to ask them.

Hi June

One of my most refreshing Messy Church visits was to a Messy Church in Nottingham on a Saturday morning. After registration, I found myself heading towards a mature lady who was on the sewing table. We were invited to make stars with embroidery thread on bookmarks. She was chatty, helpful and friendly. I asked her if she always volunteered for doing this kind of activity. She told me that she loved the variety of Messy Church and belongs to every team! She is on the activities team one month, then the kitchen team another month and the welcome table another month again. She was in her element! I dared to ask her which team she enjoyed the most. But she declared that every team was as worthwhile and equally valued, and she could have so many conversations with the team and families by volunteering in these different ways. Later, I discovered that she was renowned for her chocolate cake! So, discuss it with your team. Some may like the invitation, but others may not. Be flexible and sensitive. Let us know how you get along.

Order your next issue of *Get Messy!*

Get Messy! is published three times per year in January, May and September.
Available from: your local Christian bookshop
Online: **brfonline.org.uk/getmessy**
By phone: +44 (0)1865 319700
By post: complete the form below

A **group subscription** works when you receive five or more copies of *Get Messy!* delivered to a single address. To order postage-free, go to brfonline.org.uk/getmessy#Groupsubscriptions.

BRF

Print copies

SUBSCRIPTION (INCLUDES POSTAGE AND PACKING)	PRICE	QTY	TOTAL (£)
May 2019 to April 2020 one-year subscription (UK)	£17.40		
May 2019 to April 2020 one-year subscription (Europe)	£25.50		
May 2019 to April 2020 one-year subscription (Rest of the world)	£29.40		
SINGLE COPIES	PRICE	QTY	TOTAL (£)
Get Messy! January–April 2019	£4.50		
Get Messy! May–August 2019	£4.60		
Postage for single copies (see right)			
Donation to BRF's Messy Church			
		Total	

Title _____ First name/initials _____ Surname _____

Address _____

_____ Postcode _____

Telephone _____ Email _____

Method of payment

☐ Cheque (made payable to BRF)   ☐ MasterCard / Visa

Card no. ☐☐☐☐ ☐☐☐☐ ☐☐☐☐ ☐☐☐☐

Valid from ☐☐ ☐☐   Expires ☐☐ ☐☐   Security code* ☐☐☐

Last 3 digits on the reverse of the card

Signature _____ Date _____

ESSENTIAL IN ORDER TO PROCESS YOUR ORDER

Messy Church is part of BRF, a Registered Charity (233280)

Digital copies

Single-copy purchases of the *Get Messy!* magazine are intended for the sole use of the purchaser. If you would like to distribute digital copies to your Messy Church team, simply click the **Buy now** button on the product page and add the number of copies you need into the quantity box. The following discounts will be applied for multiple copies:

1–2 copies: no discount   3–4 copies: 10% discount
5–9 copies: 15% discount   10+ copies: 20% discount

For further information about purchasing digital copies and copyright information, see **brfonline.org.uk/terms**.

POSTAGE AND PACKING CHARGES			
Order value	UK	Europe	Rest of world
Under £7.00	£2.00	£5.00	£7.00
£7.00–£29.99	£3.00	£9.00	£15.00
£30.00+	FREE	£9.00 + 15% of order value	£15.00 + 20% of order value

General information

Delivery times within the UK are normally 15 working days. All prices are subject to the current rate of VAT. Prices are correct at the time of going to press but may change without prior notice. Offers available while stocks last.

Return this form with the appropriate payment to:

BRF, 15 The Chambers, Vineyard, Abingdon OX14 3FE
Tel. +44 (0)1865 319700   Fax +44 (0)1865 319701

To read our terms and find out about cancelling your order, please visit **brfonline.org.uk/terms**.

You can pay for your annual subscription using Direct Debit. You need only give your bank details once, and the payment is made automatically every year until you cancel it. If you would like to pay by Direct Debit, please also use the form below, entering your BRF account number under 'Reference' if you know it. You are fully covered by the Direct Debit Guarantee.

Instruction to your bank or building society to pay by Direct Debit

DIRECT Debit

Please fill in the whole form using a ballpoint pen and return it to:
BRF, 15 The Chambers, Vineyard, Abingdon OX14 3FE

Service User Number: 5 5 8 2 2 9

Name and full postal address of your bank or building society

To: The Manager	Bank/Building Society
Address	
	Postcode

Name(s) of account holder(s)

_____

Branch sort code
☐☐ – ☐☐ – ☐☐

Bank/Building Society account number
☐☐☐☐☐☐☐☐

Reference number

Instruction to your Bank/Building Society
Please pay The Bible Reading Fellowship Direct Debits from the account detailed in this instruction, subject to the safeguards assured by the Direct Debit Guarantee. I understand that this instruction may remain with The Bible Reading Fellowship and, if so, details will be passed electronically to my bank/building society.

Signature(s)

Banks and Building Societies may not accept Direct Debit instructions for some types of account.

The Direct Debit Guarantee

- This Guarantee is offered by all banks and building societies that accept instructions to pay Direct Debits.
- If there are any changes to the amount, date or frequency of your Direct Debit, The Bible Reading Fellowship will notify you 10 working days in advance of your account being debited or as otherwise agreed. If you request The Bible Reading Fellowship to collect a payment, confirmation of the amount and date will be given to you at the time of the request.
- If an error is made in the payment of your Direct Debit, by The Bible Reading Fellowship or your bank or building society, you are entitled to a full and immediate refund of the amount paid from your bank or building society.
- If you receive a refund you are not entitled to, you must pay it back when The Bible Reading Fellowship asks you to.
- You can cancel a Direct Debit at any time by simply contacting your bank or building society. Written confirmation may be required. Please also notify us.

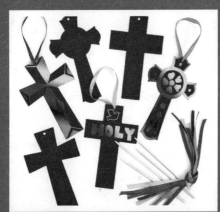